"This is a much needed, powerful resource for women who struggle with anxiety, boundaries, fear and perfectionism. Many will identify with the courageous stories shared within. I, for one, couldn't put it down! It was just what I needed."

—SHAWNA WILLIAMS

"Raw and vulnerable, courageous and unbelievably bold, *No Longer A Yes Girl* doesn't sugar coat anything. If you're dealing with depression and looking for hope, look no further."

—JOHNNA MYERS

No Longer A
Yes Girl

Editing: One Word Editing (Stacey Covell)
Publishing and Design Services: MartinPublishingServices.com

Some names and identifying details have been changed to protect the privacy of individuals.

ISBN: 978-1-7353031-0-9 (paperback)
          978-1-7353031-2-3 (epub)

No Longer A
Yes Girl

Exchanging Perfectionism,
People-Pleasing, *and* Fear
for Restorative Mental Health

RANA McINTYRE

For my girls.

I hope you always know you are never alone.

I love you both with all my heart!

Contents

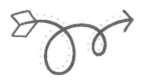

Introduction

As I journeyed into writing this book and sharing what God has done in my own life, I figured I had two options. One, I could choose to tell the truth, despite how ugly some of it may appear and trust that God will use my story to give others freedom, or I could hide in fear and risk passing this fear on to my greatest and most treasured possessions—my children. I've chosen to share my story so that my children know they are never alone. I too am imperfect, and regardless of the choices they make along the way, I want my daughters to know that no matter what they are loved, valued, and worthy.

I grew up believing a very different story. One that told me my value and worth were based on what I did and how others viewed me. As a result, I grew up performing. For many years I tried to play the role of the good daughter, sister, friend, spouse, and Christian as I believed I had to be. Through my childhood and into my adult years, I grew to believe I was the only one who struggled to live in this world as an imperfect human being. From where I stood, those around me had it all together; they were perfect, and I was not. As this belief grew and dominated my thinking, it took a toll on my brain and in return I struggled mentally and emotionally.

The darkest part of the mental health battle is the belief that no one in your circle of friends, family, church, or community has ever strayed off course. This is the last thing I ever want to do to my children. If I have learned anything through my battle with mental health, it is that we need to share the truth. When we aren't honest, we create a facade that perpetuates the myth that when we suffer—me, you, all of us—we are alone. And loneliness is such a dark place for those already struggling and believing they don't belong.

There seems to be this misconception that if we are followers of Christ we live without blemish (or at least serious ones). While this is true from the perspective of a sinner saved by grace, we each still have a history, a story, a past. Unfortunately, when we believe the Christian label is synonymous with perfection, we create even more isolation and feel like we must be the only one who is struggling and so need to hide. But this is not true. When we hide the mistakes of our past, or those of the present, it becomes very easy to live like a Pharisee, casting our judgmental glances on those whom we see, and in our isolation need to see, as somehow less than us. We puff ourselves up, point our fingers, and push people away instead of inviting others to come alongside us, walking together, and being honest about who we really are. How do I know these things? Because I used to do it too.

Thankfully, I have come to learn that I must fight fear and the voices that seek to silence me. Because to bow to fear is to only serve another god and when I do this I hand over not just myself, but also my children as victims. When I stay silent, I teach them to also stay silent. This is exactly what Satan wants. He doesn't want us to fight; he wants to keep us in silence, to keep us oppressed.

The Bible talks about the consequences however, of not suiting up to battle this war of oppression. "You shall not bow down to them [other gods] or worship them; for I, the Lord your God, am a jealous God, punishing the children for the sin of the parents to the third and fourth generation of those who hate me, but showing love to a thousand generations of those who love me and keep my commandments" (Deuteronomy 5:9-10). While I don't believe God is sitting on a pedestal waiting to punish my children, grandchildren, and great grandchildren if I get it wrong, I see that the natural consequences of my everyday actions and behaviors are what I indirectly teach to those watching me. Knowing this, I want to do my best to reflect the core principles Jesus built his ministry on—love, grace, and forgiveness. But in order to do this, I first must understand the depth of God's great love, grace, and forgiveness for myself. Then, knowing his love, grace, and forgiveness firsthand, I can extend these things more freely to those around me and disarm the enemy whose sole desire is to annihilate God's children.

When I decided to put my big idea to paper for this book, I wrote out this declaration, "This book removes the gag order and hangs the abuser on the gallows meant for those who are suffering." As I did this I was thinking of the story of Esther in the Old Testament. Orphaned at a young age and raised by her older cousin Mordecai, Esther is given a choice at a monumental point in her life. She becomes queen as the wife of King Xerxes, but keeps her Jewish nationality and family background a secret at Mordecai's wise mandate. But Haman, the king's chief advisor, issued a decree to "kill and annihilate all the Jews—young and old, women and children" after Mordecai wouldn't kneel down and pay honor to him as he had been commanded to do (Esther 3:13). Now Esther has a choice. She can hide her identity in hopes of preserving her image and safety, or she can come clean with the king, be forthright about her origin, and trust that God will be with her. So Esther asks Mordecai to gather all of the Jews in their town and says, "Fast for me. Do not eat or drink for three days, night or day. When this is done, I will go to the king, even though it is against the law. And if I perish, I perish" (4:16). Despite the risks, Esther ends up saving not only herself but an entire nation and Haman ends up being impaled and killed for what he did. Like Esther, I hope that in coming forward with my own story, it will empower and bring comfort to others who also suffer, that they will learn they are not to blame, and most of all know they are not alone.

For several years now, my husband and I have dreamed of owning a small hobby farm. But living in one of the wealthiest counties in middle Tennessee and raising a family on one income brought us to a stark realization: This dream of ours is farfetched. But in hopes of finding something, we look anyways. There usually isn't anything on the market that fits the bill, but recently a property came up that looked promising.

From the outside looking in it was in great shape. It was an all brick, two-level, Cape Cod home, with arched front windows on the lower front level and dormer windows along the porch's roof line. It had a deep three-car garage around the back connected by a breezeway, with a sunroom and floor to ceiling windows that overlooked the back pasture. Built in 1997, it sat back off the road on about ten acres of land. The front half of the property was all pasture while the back half had pasture and woods with an aging six-stall horse barn just at the start of the tree line. It was beyond our budget, but I was hopeful knowing it needed some work and believing we might be able to get a deal. When we walked into the house however, the hope of what we saw on the outside quickly faded. The musty smell made it clear that this home had not been tended to in a while. The sticky wood floors and mice feces throughout were proof that though the home appeared to be abandoned, it was still in fact, occupied. The closer we looked the more obvious the rodent infestation became. Not only were there mice and raccoon feces in the insulation of the attic and what seemed to be mice urine on the floors, but they had even made their way into the kitchen's freezer! This of course opened the question of whether the pests had infiltrated the walls of the home possibly compromising the electrical system.

Despite all of this, I remained hopeful. This was the first house we had seen that was large enough to meet the needs of our family even though it needed a lot of work on the inside. It was obvious the home would occupy my life for several months if we were to take the project on, but I was prepared to do an overhaul on it. After a lot of research, we determined the needs of the house far exceeded our pockets, and recognizing our limitations, we walked away.

I'm still thinking about that house. In fact, its story resonates so much with my own that I am not surprised by the willingness I had to dive in and make it what it could be. What I saw in that house is what God has been teaching me about my own soul—that no matter how good my life may appear from the outside, it's what's on the inside that truly matters.

The Bible tells me that my body is the Lord's temple and that I am to care for it. But that house gave me a deeper understanding. I can care for what is seen on the outside—my physical body—and make the world around me believe all is well, but if I don't take care of what is living on the inside—my soul—I am only an empty, decaying temple that is unable to provide for those around me.

Unfortunately, our society promotes the idea that our outward appearance is what matters most. As a result, many of us paint a persona and build our identity on what we hope will be accepted by those around us, whether we agree with it or not. Churches sometimes also perpetuate this myth—telling us the dos and don'ts of the Bible as they believe it to be. Sadly, in prioritizing appearances over the Gospel and Jesus's unconditional love, our behavior becomes disconnected from the heart and hypocrisy easily takes root.

Though I grew up in a home where I knew I was loved and my parents did their best to raise me with what they knew to be right and true, unconsciously I came to learn what I suspect many others did—that life is about what others see, believe, and say and not what we see, believe, or say ourselves. Desiring to be seen as good and not receive punishment for going against the rules, I worked hard to play the part just so, trying to live as perfectly as possible in order to avoid rocking the boat. I thought if I assumed the role that was expected of me without fighting, I would suffer less. I had no idea that living my life this way would one day backfire on me.

You see in never standing up for myself and speaking my own truth a different kind of harm came my way. Harm that was more detrimental to my mind, body, and spirit than standing up to any opponent would have been. All the voices of my past merged into one abusive script and swelled to an epic proportion. The internal battle that ensued made me want to die. This war eventually brought me face to face with my own mental health and taught me that what I believe about myself is vastly more important than the thoughts and opinions of others.

Because of my journey through trauma, tragedy, and hardship, I know it's time to write this book and share my story. A story that shows why retreating and hiding is not the way to life. A story that shares how looking good on the outside for acceptance is detrimental, not only to ourselves, but also to those we love. This is my story, and despite my fears, I'm taking a step of faith. I'm drawing back the curtains and revealing the truth about the girl you see so that you may know there is more to me, and more to you, than what meets the eye. No matter the outcome, God loves me, sees me, knows me, and accepts me. God sees you, knows you, and accepts you too. Whatever your story is, I pray that the words of this book will remind you, and us all, that life isn't about how we portray ourselves to the world around us but it's what comes when we live authentically from the inside out.

If pleasing people were my goal, I would not be Christ's servant.

GALATIANS 1:10

Chapter 1

When Tragedy Hit

THREE YEARS INTO MARRIAGE, MY HUSBAND AND I conceived and nine months later I gave birth to a beautiful baby girl. She changed our lives. Everything about her was perfect. For three months I got to stay home with her. It was heaven on earth. But the day came when I had to face reality and return to work. I arranged childcare through my close friend, Tiffany. She was a stay-at-home mom with a toddler and had just had her second baby, a couple of months before me.

Tiffany wasn't quite ready to start the childcare when my maternity leave was over, so I found another friend to watch my daughter in the meantime. A few weeks later Tiffany assured me she was ready to take on the role of being my daughter's primary babysitter, so we moved forward with our plans. Tiffany's house was conveniently located between home and the office, so this made dropping my baby girl off in the morning and picking her up in the afternoon ideal. I missed being home with my daughter, but knowing she was with a good friend made it more bearable.

Around two months later, I left the office at the end of my workday and drove to my friend's house to pick up my daughter. It was a cold January day. By now we had settled into a normal routine. As I arrived at the house and walked inside, I immediately knew something was wrong. My daughter was making strange noises I had never heard before. Unlike every other day, where I would get her into her snowsuit and place her into the baby carrier when I arrived, today she was already bundled in her snowsuit and in the carrier ready to go. When I asked about the abnormal sounds she was making my friend told me she was probably just dreaming as she slept.

Unnerved by this unusual behavior, I unfastened her straps and started to get her out of her carrier to see what might be going on. As I lifted her from the carrier, she projectile vomited all over me. Something was very wrong. I frantically took off her snowsuit attempting to wake her up, but she was listless and continued making the strange noises. This was not the same baby I knew. I quickly cleaned her as best I could, put her back into her car seat, picked it up, said goodbye to my friend, and walked out the door to the car. As I drove out of the driveway, I called my husband, who was already home from work and then I called the doctor.

A similar incident had occurred over a week before, except that day Tiffany called me at work. I left early to pick my baby girl up thinking she must have some sort of a bug. I called the pediatrician to see if I should bring her in and they recommended I watch her for a couple of hours and call back if anything changed. I stayed with her at my friend's and we talked for a couple of hours while she slept in my arms. Eventually I loaded her into the car seat and headed out.

Because it had been a couple of hours and she was still asleep, I decided to stop by another friend's house. Her husband was an ER doctor and I wanted to get his opinion on the situation. She had a history of bladder reflux—it landed us in the ER when she was four weeks old—so I wanted to make sure this wasn't somehow connected. The babysitter had told me she hadn't eaten much that day. I told this to the doctor, and he recommended I try to feed her. After I finished feeding her though, within fifteen minutes she projectile vomited everything she had taken in.

The doctor recommended I call her pediatrician immediately, which I did, and he even spoke with the pediatrician himself to tell her what he was seeing. The pediatrician recommended we watch her for a couple more hours and then give her some Pedialyte a little later on. So we went home, and my husband and I continued to monitor her. We gave her the Pedialyte that evening, but she threw up again. Still concerned, I called the pediatrician once more and she recommended we take her to the emergency room.

While we were in the E.R. she was fussy and the doctor carried her around at the hospital, trying to console her and gently stroking the top of her head. They also did chest and belly X-rays. After looking everything over they concluded our girl probably had a virus and as she started to come around a little, they gave us the all clear to go home. Within twenty-four hours she seemed more like herself and was given a clean bill of health the next day at her six-month doctor's appointment.

Now that the same thing was happening a second time, I was more concerned. It wasn't like my baby girl to be so lethargic and have symptoms of vomiting for no reason, especially two weeks in a row. The doctor told me she would call me in two hours to check on her and if she wasn't any better by then, we would take her to the emergency room since it was past regular office hours. The next couple of hours were concerning. No matter what I did she would not open her eyes. She looked like she was asleep, but she continued whimpering and making sounds she'd never made before. If I tried to lay her down, she would begin to cry which also was different from her normal behavior. The only way I could console her was to hold her.

Over the next two hours my husband and I took turns trying to console her while we waited for the next call from the doctor. We racked our brains, trying to think of what might be causing her to get sick like this. We wondered if there was undetected mold in our house or the babysitter's house. We questioned if she might be having a severe reaction to her formula or if she had been exposed to a virus. Maybe the bladder reflux was causing a problem again. We had no clue what was going on, so one by one, I spoke with several close friends and family members over the phone, recounting the days, trying to figure out why our baby was so sick. No one had any initial ideas either. But my father called me back a while after we first spoke.

He told me something strong had come over him and he felt he needed to say something. He was concerned the two occurrences were related and there was a connection between our daughter's illness and her babysitter. I pushed it aside, thinking why would that even enter his mind? After all this was my friend. We grew up together; I had known her for years. It seemed asinine. But when the doctor called to check in, I mentioned my father's concern and asked her if she saw any correlation between the two episodes. Suddenly the doctor's voice changed.

"Take the baby to the hospital right now," she said.

Once we got to the ER we were taken back to a private room where we explained what was going on, our concerns about the two incidents and wondering if they were related, and explained that our pediatrician told us to come in for an MRI. The staff agreed and went ahead with the imaging. Additionally they asked if they could also get some X-rays. Wanting answers, we didn't bat an eye, we just said okay.

Right before the X-ray, while we were still in the hallway waiting to go into the X-ray room she began to seize while my husband was holding her. Terrified, we both started yelling for help unsure of what was going on. Some staff came to help and after a little while her tiny frame stopped shaking and they were able to take the X-rays. We went back to our room to wait for the results and while we waited, she had two more seizures.

After what seemed like forever, several medical personnel crowded into the room. They gave us the results of the CT scan and explained that it showed signs of both old and new blood on the brain which was likely the result of her being shaken multiple times. The doctors explained that the next several hours were critical because they didn't know if or when the bleeding would stop. As we started asking questions about the situation and possible outcomes, they admitted to us that they didn't know if she would survive or not.

I didn't understand what the doctors were telling us. Someone mentioned the babysitter and shaken baby syndrome, but I didn't know what shaken baby syndrome was. Desperately trying to wrap my mind around what we had just been told, I immediately internalized the news. Was I somehow responsible? Was this somehow my fault? Everything was happening so fast. We didn't know what to do, all we knew was that something was terribly wrong with our baby.

Doctors and nurses started bombarding us with questions. The case was now a child abuse case, they said.

Everyone who had been with our daughter that day was a suspect. I was terrified. What time did I drop her off at the babysitter's? How was she when I dropped her off? When did I pick her up? When did I call the doctor? Was she showing symptoms when I arrived at the babysitter's house after work? They seemed to focus on the babysitter but question after question, I answered the best I could, recounting the day with each and every person she had been with.

In the whirlwind of activity, we were also told our daughter needed to be transferred to the intensive care unit downtown and that we would need to go by ambulance. They said I could ride along in the ambulance, and that my husband could follow behind. As I sat in the passenger seat of the ambulance, I had no control. My mind couldn't process everything that was happening—they were telling us the babysitter was likely at fault given the time frame of events—I was too consumed with blaming myself. Here I was only a few feet from my baby girl, and I couldn't hold her or comfort her. I kept looking back at her wondering if she was going to be okay, while berating myself, still believing this was all my fault, even though the doctors were telling us otherwise.

Once we arrived at the intensive care unit a new set of doctors questioned us again (as it was their job to do) about the hours leading up to bringing her to the hospital. Because I was the one who had picked her up earlier that evening from the babysitter's house, I was questioned over and over about each and every detail. Over the next twenty-four hours my husband and I were both interrogated, not only by the doctors, but also by police officers at the hospital and Child Protective Services (CPS). The babysitter was also later questioned and soon after that was arrested and charged with battery resulting in serious bodily injury.

The midnight hours turned into morning. It felt like we were in the middle of a horrible nightmare with our sweet baby girl. My husband and I asked every single medical provider that walked through the doors of the NICU (Neonatal Intensive Care Unit), what was going to happen to our precious daughter. None of them could give a straight answer only that the next thirty-six hours would be critical. So hour by hour we waited. And waited. And waited.

Thirty-six hours came and went and over the next week, little by little, she began to show signs of improvement. The blood on her brain began to recede without further treatment and she slowly regained consciousness.

Testing and imaging continued throughout the week and as doctors put more pieces together, they shared their findings with us.

They told us they found a bruise on her jaw line, as well as retinal hemorrhaging in both eyes. This made it clear she had been shaken, severely. Given the bruise they found on her jaw line, they told us that she was likely shaken around the throat. They also had to put her on a feeding tube since she was still unconscious. Additional testing confirmed she had also lost the ability to swallow without aspirating her food—a common side effect of brain damage and a skill she would have to relearn through intense therapy.

A variety of medical specialists and therapists, including a pediatric ophthalmologist, visited daily. He told us her vision was severely impaired as a result of the blood behind her eyes. He explained that as the blood cleared, hopefully her vision would too, but cautioned us that there was no guarantee there wouldn't be permanent damage. Within a week we were transferred from the NICU, to a regular floor and started to comprehend the weight of the damage to her brain.

Chapter 2

How Did I Get Here? My Story

From the time I was little I learned and believed that life is about what you do and how people perceive you. Though I knew the only being to walk this earth without sin was Jesus, I still struggled. I couldn't reconcile that sin was still a part of being human. In my mind sin was bad, and if I sinned, then I was also bad. I couldn't accept my sinful, human self with the societal and Christian standards put before me. So I did what many do—I lived two lives. The life expected of me for the sake of approval and the life of a scared, lonely, imperfect girl wanting to be loved for who she was, not what she did or didn't do.

Growing up, I attended a small, rural, public school where everyone knew our family. Being the child of a middle school grammar teacher and high school biology teacher in the same school district, expectations were set a little higher for me. After all, they were public figures in our community. I can only imagine this added to the standard they were also held to, desiring to be seen as citizens who were not only good in the eyes of the community, but also as parents raising rule-abiding kids.

Between church and school, I grew up living as I was taught, being a good, upstanding, Christian girl. I behaved in school. I walked through our church doors every Sunday morning and evening, and for every midweek service. I went to Sunday school, was active in our youth group, sang during Sunday morning worship services, and was part of the choir. I did and said all the right things. I had learned the part well and I played it perfectly.

In order to make it as a Christian and maintain my right standing within the community at large, one had to play by the rules. If you drank, did drugs, had or even talked about sex, you were bad. You submitted to authority and did as you were told, no questions asked. You were the company you kept, and if any anger was directed at you it was because you messed up and disobeyed. "Spare the rod and spoil the child" was the rhetoric of the day. I now see the problem with this is that a person's anger is not always someone else's fault, but it took me years to learn this truth.

Around second grade, my class held a spelling bee. As we all stood in front of the empty desk chairs, my friend Lily was first. I was nervous for her. The class collectively leaned in to see if she could spell "ANSWER." I really wanted her to spell her word correctly. I even crossed my fingers in hope. But suddenly my teacher paused the spelling bee and pointed at my hand.

"Rana? What are you doing?"

"Hoping Lily spells the word right."

"No you're not. You're trying to sign Lily the letters. You're trying to get her to cheat," she replied. I wasn't, but the teacher didn't believe me, end of story. She told me to sit down; I was eliminated from the spelling bee.

Then there was the day I walked into the school bathroom looking for my speech teacher. I attended a speech therapy class once a week to work on my "R" sounds. On this day, like many before, I climbed the stairs to the upper level classroom where my speech class was, but my teacher was nowhere to be found. So, I sat down in the classroom and waited for her. There were only a couple of rooms on the upper level of the old school building I attended, and the girl's bathroom was tucked into a corner just across the hall from her room. After sitting there for a few minutes, and curious if my teacher knew I was waiting on her, I walked across the hallway to see if she was in the bathroom.

As I walked in I saw her walking to the sink from the bathroom stall. I began to tell her I was looking for her but before I could get any words out, she glared and started yelling at me, "What are you doing in here Rana? Get out of here!"

I quickly turned and ran back to her room. I was so confused. I didn't know why she yelled at me. I didn't know what I had done wrong.

I also had trouble in fourth grade. My teacher did not like me. I made a comment one day walking into the classroom after we had all come in from recess. I don't remember what I said, but I know I wasn't being disrespectful. The next thing I knew, she grabbed onto a chunk of my hair and in front of the whole classroom, told the other students that if I were her daughter, she would pull my hair for the comment I had made. Needless to say, time and time again I learned it was vital to walk the straight and narrow!

Middle school brought another set of circumstances. By sixth grade I was boy crazy. I had "boyfriends" here and there but nothing serious. Most boys from my school wouldn't date me since I was the daughter of two school-teachers, but church was always a viable option. When I was eleven and still in sixth grade, I was "dating," which really only meant I saw him at youth functions, a boy in eighth grade. Because I ran with him and his friends—the older kids of the group—I was encouraged by the girls to let him kiss me. "It's no big deal," they said. I thought about what they said and thought they had a point; it really wasn't a big deal. I also didn't want him to not like me, and so, I had my first kiss.

Sadly, it didn't stop there. One night, our youth group was riding home from a youth event in the church van. My boyfriend and I were sitting next to each other and his arm was around my waist. As we rode along in the dark, I suddenly felt his hand making its way into my shorts. I froze. I didn't understand what was happening or know what to do, so I stayed motionless and quiet as he found his way around and into me. It hurt, but I didn't say a thing. I just waited for it to be over and acted like nothing happened. I had no vocabulary or understanding for what transpired in the darkness of that van ride, I only knew it didn't feel good, it was sexual, and sex wasn't something to talk about. This was the beginning of my understanding of what men wanted from me, and it shaped much of my thinking and actions moving forward.

High school brought its own struggles as I tried to navigate the waters of what it meant to be a "good Christian girl" through the eyes of my parents and those watching me. The stakes and standards were high. This became crystal clear during my freshman year when a false rumor started going around school about me.

It was a Friday night and there was a home football game. I was dating a senior; the one brave student who didn't care that my father was a teacher. For no particular reason, we left the stadium to sit in his truck in the school parking lot during the halftime performance. I laid my head down in his lap with my face looking up at him while we were talking to each other. Some friends stopped by, poking their heads into the open windows to talk to us as well. It was harmless fun. But the tone quickly changed as I made my way from his truck back into the stadium bleachers for the second half of the game and realized I was the talk of the student body. One of his friends who had stopped by the truck took it upon himself to tell anyone willing to listen that I had just given my boyfriend a blowjob.

The next several days were excruciating. From riding home with my father that evening, where he served as a linesman at the game, wondering if he had heard the rumor, to facing the question "Did you really give him a blowjob?" all day at school on Monday. Every moment was awful. But the worst thing of all happened Monday after school.

Every day after school I walked to the back hallway of the school to get a coke and a candy bar from the snack machines. After that I would walk to my father's classroom and wait for him to finish up his work for the day. Then we would pick up my mom from work at the middle school and head home. We did the same thing every day.

On this Monday, when I turned to walk to my father's classroom and he was walking toward me, I felt it in my gut. He knew. As I made my way toward him, he turned away from me without saying a word. I was silent. It didn't really surprise me that he'd heard the rumor since I had been bombarded with it all day from my classmates, but his silence was deafening, and I was scared. It seemed like he must have believed what he'd heard or he wouldn't have come searching for me.

After we got home, my mom left the house to run some errands and I sat down to practice the piano. I was hoping to sidestep this whole uncomfortable ordeal, but was soon interrupted by a tap on my shoulder.

"Come and sit down at the table with me," he said. I stopped playing and followed him into our dining room, sitting down at the table across from him. I was nervous and uncomfortable.

He pulled out a piece of paper and laid it in front of me. "Read this," He said. I picked it up and began reading. It was a letter detailing the false rumor about me at school. There was no signature, only initials. When I finished reading I looked up at my father who was watching me. I felt sick. "What happened on Friday night?" he asked.

I explained that during the halftime show we went out to my boyfriend's truck to hang out and how I laid my head down in his lap while we were talking with friends. I told him that was it. "Nothing happened, Dad," I said. Telling him about my evening was difficult and uncomfortable because these were not regular conversations in our home; it was so embarrassing and scary. I didn't know if my dad believed what I was saying. I wondered why someone would even write this about me. What did I do to deserve this?

After I finished telling him everything, including what didn't happen, we sat there for a moment. Then he said, "I want to believe you, but I don't." He went on to tell me he wasn't going to share any of this with my mother because it would be too upsetting for her. I didn't understand why he wasn't going to share anything with her when I hadn't done anything wrong, but I just sat there and said nothing, wanting the conversation to end. After he finished telling me we weren't going to tell my mom, he got up and left the room and that was it. I felt a lot of shame.

I didn't understand why my dad didn't believe me. I didn't do anything wrong. I told the full truth and withheld nothing. But at that moment, it didn't matter. I was still at fault in his eyes and the blame felt heavy on my shoulders.

When Tuesday morning came, as we walked into the school together he asked, "Are you ready for today?"

"Yes," I said, wondering why he was even asking. I had already been fighting this beast for four days on my own, how was today going to be any different?

In my junior year I auditioned for the school talent show at my high school. It was an event I looked forward to every year. I loved the feeling of being on stage and the creative outlet music gave me. Desiring to be in front of an audience as much as possible, I chose to audition for two spots in the show. First, performing a solo to a fun, upbeat Christian song and then singing a duet with a friend to a secular song. The auditions seemed to go well, but afterwards the technical director who was a teacher at the school judging the auditions asked me how I could try out singing both a secular song and a Christian song in the same show. My heart sank. I felt ashamed. I didn't have an answer though, so I didn't say anything in response. Once again, I had somehow done something wrong, but I still didn't know what.

By this time, what started as a little whisper as a child had grown bigger and louder. It told me my actions—or perceived actions—were what defined me. It told me that good people do things right and bad people do things wrong; there is no middle ground, no in between. After being molested I allowed others to do things to me, with the lies being cemented that I was only as valuable as what I did and what others saw and accepted. I felt a lot of guilt and shame. However, the desire of being wanted and chosen, even if it was for something temporary, was far stronger than being okay with no one choosing me and being alone. I now understand that my actions, behaviors, and choices were all a part of a belief that had taken hold in my mind. I wasn't worthy of real love and my only good characteristics were visible ones.

By the time I got to college, I struggled to believe God loved me for me. My entire life had taught me it's what you do that matters, not who you are. Since I knew I had done plenty of things that weren't perfect I was sure God was angry at me. Even though I professed to be a Christian and even attended a Christian university, internally I constantly questioned my right standing with God.

One weekend, my parents came to visit me at school and we went for a bite to eat at the local Applebee's. While we were there, my older sister (also a student at the same school) and I were having a discussion about God and heaven and I asked her if she thought I would go to heaven or not. I wanted her to tell me yes, she thought I would. I needed her affirmation because I truly didn't know if God would allow me into heaven if I died. I knew he saw both sides of me and I wasn't living up to the standards I believed I needed to be. To me, God was punitive, a punishing God, and I was scared of him. I felt like if my act wasn't together and I was killed in a car accident, I better be prayed up, because if I wasn't, he was going to send me to hell. She affirmed me as only a sister can, assuring me I wouldn't be going to hell.

After making it through college I got engaged. We were best friends. I loved my soon-to-be husband and he loved me. We spent every bit of time we had together and believed we were bound for a life of goodness. We were so happy when our wedding day arrived, but by our first anniversary we were struggling. I hated sex. He loved sex. I couldn't figure out what was wrong with me. After all, it was my duty and responsibility. It was what I was supposed to do. I kept thinking: *What is wrong with you Rana? Married couples have sex. This is how God intended it to be.*

Once again, I was struggling to live up to the belief that it was my job to satisfy my husband's desires. It never occurred to me that it wasn't my responsibility to make him happy, or that his reactions to me were based out of his own insecurities and shame, just as mine were to him. Standing up for myself and saying "no" only made him mad. I was damned if I did, damned if I didn't. Either way, it was my fault. Trying to take the path of least resistance, I did what was asked of me. I didn't want to feel as though I was bad because I couldn't give him what he wanted. I wanted to be good. So I did my best to put on my "good, married, Christian wife hat," even though I still always felt I came up short. Many fights ensued, and many tears were shed.

I felt doomed. I yearned for approval. I had spent years trying so hard to be accepted by everyone around me who seemed to do life so perfectly. But what I didn't realize was that in this yearning and striving I had lost my own standards. Heck, I didn't even know what my standards were. All I knew was that it was my duty to keep everyone happy. No matter the damage being done to me along the way. Look the part. Keep the peace. Shut your mouth and be a good girl. At. Any. Cost.

Chapter 3

Life After What Happened

THE DAYS, WEEKS, MONTHS, AND YEARS THAT PASSED after what happened to our sweet baby girl tortured me. I did everything I could to find answers; to relieve myself of carrying the weight of this burden. At the beginning, I even spoke with Tiffany who, despite her arrest and charge, denied the accusations, and responded to me saying, "That's silly, who would shake her?"

I really wanted to believe her. This was my friend. We grew up together and went to the same college. We even went to the same church. We used to be inseparable. This wasn't just an ordinary friendship, we had history. Wanting so badly to believe her, my family and I did more research, searching and looking for something, anything, that could possibly explain what had happened to my sweet little girl. But even the research still left us with only one conclusion. Based on her interview with the detective, along with the medical staff's training and expertise, she was responsible. Her denial, however, left the door open in my brain as to what happened that day—both days—to my little girl and so, despite doing nothing wrong, I took on the burden. I suffered tremendous loss and heartache over my daughter's trauma and the circumstances around it.

After my daughter was diagnosed with shaken baby syndrome I suffered mentally. For the first two years after the injury as we waited for the case to go to trial, I attempted to resume life. But everything about my life had changed. I left my job at a recording studio to stay home with my daughter to provide the necessary care she now needed. A multitude of appointments with neurologists, ophthalmologists, and a variety of occupational and physical therapists became my new normal. My husband and I couldn't bear to go to church and deal with the questions and glances, or risk running into Tiffany. I stopped singing with the Christian quartet I had recorded and traveled with since before getting married. I could no longer sing of hope, love, or joy; mine had all been stolen. Joy was a thing of the past as we struggled to cope.

I fell into a deep depression and also began suffering severe anxiety. I struggled to sleep and function for months. I would wake up in the middle of the night fixated on one thought—I was responsible. I needed and yearned for an answer to what specifically happened to my daughter, but I didn't have it. I only had the remains of what happened, and the facts given to me by every medical provider we encountered, but unfortunately the one person who was with her that day wouldn't give me any more answers.

I wrestled with thoughts of suicide, though no one was aware because I hid it well. The thrill of being a new mom was gone. Being home all day with my baby was frightening. What if something else happened to her? I would definitely be responsible then, I thought. Little things that happened would send me calling for immediate help. If she was sitting in her baby pillow and lightly bumped her head when she tipped over, I would call the doctor, terrified that any little bump would cause more brain damage.

My new world felt dark. I was isolated and scared. This created the ideal environment for my accuser, Satan, to place doubt within my mind. It tormented me. Unable to stop what was going on inside, I grappled to cope, and unconsciously began doing what I could to control my surroundings. I stopped watching television, reading the news, or listening to secular radio. It seemed like everywhere I turned stories of shaken baby syndrome were popping up.

One day during this period, Julie, a close friend of mine asked me to attend a Beth Moore Bible study with her at the church. I didn't want to attend. It was still too soon for me to go back to church and I didn't want to bump into Tiffany. So, Julie brought the study materials, videos, and a workbook to me. Needing something to help me through this time, I decided to pop one of the VHS tapes in just to see what the study was about. As I listened to Beth speak, a sense of comfort enveloped me, so I decided I would do the study. They were intense, hour-long sessions. But every day I worked through more pages of the workbook, devouring the information.

Desperately wanting to stop my mental torment I worked hard to fill myself with nothing but God. I was sure he was punishing me for my imperfections. My sins had caught up with me and I was facing the consequences. In my mind, my daughter's injuries and now my own self-blame was God's judgement on me and my sins. Desiring to be good and wanting to be viewed as right in his eyes, I tried. This was the beginning of me seeking release from the mental strongholds that were holding me captive.

Realizing we needed a fresh start, my husband and I sold our house, the one we bought and renovated as new-lyweds. We weren't quite ready to purchase another home at this point, so we moved into a rental property in the town where we grew up. It was significantly closer to our families, but about an hour from the community we had come to call home. After we moved, I continued trying to fill my mind with nothing more than God's word through a multitude of self-help books and Christian studies. They became the food I used to fill the dark, empty space within me. As soon as I finished one study, I found myself back at the Christian bookstore searching for anything I could find to help me. Beth Moore, Joyce Meyer, and evangelist T.D. Jakes helped soothe my troubled mind. If I wasn't reading their books, I was searching for their shows on the television. I became obsessed. I needed to either be watch-ing them on television, reading their books, or listening to Christian music. If I wasn't doing these things, I was reading my Bible day in and day out. It honestly became like a drug for me. The more intensely I suffered, the more I devoured anything they had to say, desperately desiring freedom from the torment going on inside my brain.

I learned a lot about spiritual warfare over those two years as we waited for the impending trial. I learned how I needed to re-wallpaper the walls of my mind with God's word and take my thoughts captive, and I learned that it was important for me to only think on good things, which wasn't easy at all. I learned that Satan was a constant enemy who sought to take me, and everyone around me, down.

I inhaled everything I was learning and took it to heart. As I read God's word and went through these studies, certain Bible verses would pop off the page at me. When they did, I'd write them down. Eventually I had a stack of index cards, so I hole-punched them, secured them together with a ring, and carried those cards with me everywhere I went. Whenever my thoughts tormented me, I pulled out my cards and spoke those scriptures over myself. I ate, drank, and slept with those cards in hopes they would heal me and my broken mind. But it wasn't enough.

Despite all the work I was doing—reading God's word, memorizing scripture, and working to overcome this one reoccurring thought—I still suffered. Guilt, sadness, and shame permeated my existence without ceasing. I tried, I always tried, but my efforts were not enough to free me from the daily torture I heard from inside my brain. I was still horrible. I was still bad. Regardless of doing all the "right things," I still wanted to die.

I knew something had to change. Around this same time an opportunity presented itself. My childhood pastor unexpectedly called me telling me I had come to mind for a job. He asked if I would design and create a multi-page brochure to communicate a proposed new building plan to their congregation. Even though I didn't have a computer with the necessary software to do the work, I jumped at the opportunity. I needed something to look forward to and this would be another way I could refocus my mind. After saying yes, I reached out to my previous employer, located an hour's drive away, and asked if I could use their computers after regular office hours. When they gave me the green light, I dove headfirst into the project.

Thinking through this new project, driving an hour to and from the office, and creating the brochure took up a lot of mental space. For the first time since my daughter's injury, I found myself experiencing relief. Finally, my mind had something else to obsess over. I couldn't help but think that maybe this was my ticket out of the mental prison I was living in.

Once I recognized the positive impact design work had on me, I began seeking it like a drug, not wanting to go back to that dark place I had been in. I eventually finished that job and decided to use the income to purchase my own computer and design software so I could continue taking on creative projects and work toward building a freelance design business.

Things seemed to be getting better. We bought a new home and moved out of our rental. We found a new church and I threw myself into it. I auditioned for the worship team, joined the choir, attended Bible studies, and began volunteering as a graphic designer with the church's communication's team. I was moving forward. I still struggled from time to time, but found work to be a sufficient distraction. So I focused on that. I worked hours on end for little to no pay. While I thought I was selflessly volunteering at church and working to get a freelance business off the ground, I was really working to keep the voices inside at bay. And it worked, for a while.

The trial came and went. It ended in a hung jury and though we had the opportunity to retry the case, I didn't want to. I just wanted the whole thing to be over. I still didn't have the closure I desired, but rehashing it wasn't going to do me any good. So, once again, we attempted to move on with our lives.

Now that we had our own home, a new church family, and the trial behind us, we were ready to have another little one. So we tried and conceived again. Almost three years after our first daughter's trauma, we welcomed our second daughter into the world. Though I thought I was on the mend from everything we had endured, things were different this time around. Instead of feeling the deep love and excitement when they placed my daughter on my chest after delivering her, the only thing I could think was: *This isn't my daughter.* Since I had heard that moms often have a different experience with their second child than they do with their first, I chalked my thoughts up to that, things were just different this time around.

However, years later I learned that the trauma we went through with our first daughter had rewired my brain. This rewiring had one job—to protect me at all costs. So when my second daughter was born, this unconscious mechanism kicked in and I disassociated with my baby girl. It said, "If you get close to her you're going to suffer more pain, like you did before." This was the beginning of my struggle with Post Traumatic Stress Disorder.

Once we were home with the baby, I was terrified something traumatic would happen to our newborn like it did before. The fear was consuming. Wanting to stop anymore hurt from coming our way, I decided to take matters into my own hands. If I couldn't keep my kids from getting hurt, I'd do the next best thing. I'd stop any more babies from being born. I begged my husband to have a vasectomy. I told him it wasn't a good idea for me to have any more children, citing the fact that I had suffered seizures in and around both of their births. He didn't want to have one, but I pushed for it regardless.

Even as we made our way to the doctor's office where the procedure was performed, we were listing out the pros and cons. My list was longer. It had to be, because I needed to be in control. So, he went through with the surgery. I remember coming home and looking at my girls and thinking: *This is our family*. I was so glad I was able to stop any more harm from coming my way.

A few years later a position within my husband's company became available in Nashville, Tennessee. He got the job, and we moved. Five years had passed since our daughter suffered her traumatic brain injury and our little girls were now three and five years old. We were glad to be in a new place and did all the necessary tasks to get settled in: we found a pediatrician, therapists for our older daughter, and specialists in a variety of fields to help us meet her needs.

I also relocated the design company I had started. My focus was solely on helping independent musicians brand themselves. With Nashville's music scene, the city was a natural fit. Having been around the industry for a while as an independent artist, and previously working as a studio manager, I knew this was an area where many needed help. What I wasn't prepared for however, was how the music industry was in the middle of a drastic change moving from physical product sales toward digital music. Though I worked endless hours to secure work and market my abilities, it quickly became obvious this was nothing more than a rotating wheel I was tirelessly trying to spin with little return on my time and investment. So, at God's prompting, I laid it down, and finally focused on being a mom.

But since work had really been a smokescreen for my pain, it wasn't long before all hell broke loose and it became clear that I was still broken in a really bad way. Dark and negative thoughts returned, crippling me to the point of not being able to breathe. I wanted to die. The thoughts kept progressing from bad to worse over the next couple of years, becoming increasingly disturbing. Intrusive and unexpected, they came as I unloaded the dishwasher or put away laundry; they came when I held my daughter; they came when we were on family vacations. They berated me day in and day out without ceasing. Still, I tried to cope. I tried to push them away. But the more I tried, the more fixated I became on the intrusive thought. I believed that good people didn't have thoughts like this. Even after all of my efforts and work, I was still bad.

So many thoughts ran through my mind. *How can I tell anyone about these thoughts inside my head? What will they think of me? Will I be put into an insane asylum? Will they call the police? Will they think I am capable of such acts? Will they think I'm an awful person too?* I was so scared I didn't feel like I could tell my husband or any of my friends. I was breaking down. It was awful and I was all alone.

My mind was attacking me and hurting me like never before. I desperately needed help. I had heard about a counselor from some of the ladies in my church. I knew nothing about her beyond how she had helped them through various situations. As I sat on my couch one day, unable to breathe and focused on the thoughts that entered my mind, I picked up the phone, dialed the number to the church, and made my first appointment. I had no idea what the future held. I only knew that everything I was trying to do on my own was getting me nowhere.

WHAT HAS *happened* TO ME *will turn out* *for* MY *deliverance.*

PHILIPPIANS 1:19

Chapter 4

Fear

"WHEN WE DENY OUR STORIES AND DISENGAGE FROM tough emotions, they don't go away; instead, they own us, they define us. Our job is not to deny the story, but to defy the ending—to rise strong, recognize our story, and rumble with the truth until we get to a place where we think, Yes. This is what happened. This is my truth. And I will choose how this story ends."[1] This quote from Brené Brown has really spoken to me over these last few years.

Prior to doing the hard work of understanding the thinking that shaped my daily actions, I lived my life

---

1 Brené Brown, *Rising Strong: How the Ability to Reset Transforms the Way We Live, Love, Parent, and Lead* (New York: Random House Trade Paperbacks, 2017), 50.

trying to measure up. As I continued to live out of my distorted thinking, I was shackled, imprisoned by my own unrealistic expectations. My day to day actions, thoughts, and beliefs kept me from fully living life as the being I was designed to be. But when I began to challenge the records playing over and over in my mind and question their validity things began to change. However, doing this required facing a giant obstacle. Fear.

Fear often comes packaged with promises of safety and comfort, but fear lies to us. Fear binds and gags us and ultimately steals life. This is why it's so important not to make decisions out of fear. Over time this has become one of the biggest lessons I have learned in my life. Why is it so vital that we don't make decisions out of fear? Because when we do, the enemy wins. Take for example, Adam and Eve.

When God created Adam and Eve and put them in the garden, everything was perfect. There was no fear, there was no shame, there were no lies. They had perfect communion with God and one another. They had free reign in the garden, with one exception, "you must not eat from the tree of the knowledge of good and evil, for when you eat from it you will certainly die" (Genesis 2:16-17). So Adam and Eve lived in the garden God had created for them and "Adam and his wife were both naked, and they felt no shame" (v. 25). But the story continues:

> Now the serpent was more crafty than any of the wild animals the Lord God had made. He said to the woman, "Did God really say, 'You must not eat from any tree in the garden'?" The woman said to the serpent, "We may eat fruit from the trees in the garden, but God did say, 'You must not eat fruit from the tree that is in the middle of the garden, and you must not touch it, or you will die.'"
>
> "You will not certainly die," the serpent said to the woman. "For God knows that when you eat from it your eyes will be opened, and you will be like God, knowing good and evil."
>
> When the woman saw that the fruit of the tree was good for food and pleasing to the eye, and also desirable for gaining wisdom, she took some and ate it. She also gave some to her husband, who was with her, and he ate it. (3:1-6).

The serpent planted a seed of doubt in Eve's mind, asking her, "Did God *really* say . . . ?" and Eve, instead of trusting God's judgement, chose to listen to the voice of doubt.

After Adam and Eve ate from the tree, several things occurred. Their disobedience led to shame (the awareness they were naked) and guilt which prompted them to cover their nakedness with fig leaves (v. 7) and then, when they heard God coming, they hid from him in fear (vv. 8–10). When God asked them why they hid, instead of owning up to what they had done, they took their fear and shame and threw it onto another, denying responsibility for their actions. Adam blamed Eve saying, "The woman you put here with me—she gave me some fruit from the tree, and I ate it." (v. 12) and Eve blamed the serpent, "The serpent deceived me, and I ate." (v. 13).

Now in this situation our human thinking expects God to do what most parents do when children disobey and punish Adam and Eve for their disobedience. But before he told them what the consequences of their actions would be, God first cursed the serpent. Seeing this allowed me to recognize God's grace toward me and all of his children, and also recognize the true culprit, Satan. God saw right to the source, saying to Satan, "Because you have done this,

'Cursed are you above all livestock and all wild animals! You will crawl on your belly and you will eat dust all the days of your life. And I will put enmity between you and the woman, and between your offspring and hers; he will crush your head, and you will strike his heel'" (v. 14-15).

Even though Adam and Eve had everything they needed in Eden, the most perfect place, they still had a choice. So when they chose to go their own way and listen to the voice of doubt over God, the consequences were unavoidable. God banished them from the garden. Adam and Eve no longer had complete intimacy and perfect relationship with the Lord; they now lived with pain—the pain of childbirth, the pain of working a cursed ground, the pain of living with sin and all its effects.

Like Eve, when we question God's love and goodness and listen to the whisper that tells us we will find life in and through outward things like beauty, success, or status, we sell ourselves short. In doubting God's unique design for our lives, we suffer in shame. Then, recognizing our nakedness we feel guilt and hide in fear. Without even knowing what we are doing, we often blame others, unable or refusing to recognize the destruction that has occurred within our own hearts. It happens so quickly.

Fear is interesting. On one hand we are given fear as a way to flee dangerous circumstances such as a house fire or an unexpected encounter with a bear. It is a natural feeling given to us to remind us to seek wisdom in difficult times and through hard decisions. However, oftentimes we let fear control us and in that fear we do what we can to control the world around us to feel safer. We might push our ideas onto others with the expectation they will do what we tell them to do. Or we might find ourselves on the other side of the stick making ourselves subservient to others because we have come to learn that raising any sort of a challenge will come back to hurt us. In fear, we use it to control our surroundings and get what we want or allow it to keep us from being everything we were made to be—all in the name of feeling safe.

But there is a line we cross when we use fear to control those around us, our livelihood, and sense of safety instead of using it to seek wisdom. It casts God out of the picture and we become susceptible to the lies of Satan which is the last thing we are actually seeking. In our minds we believe that the only way to find protection is to push away anything and everything that is contrary to what we believe or bow to others and what they believe. When we let fear rule like this, we lose a vital element of God's law: faith.

I have personally experienced both sides of fear. I have been the person trying to control the world around me, living a legalistic lifestyle demanding others to bow to my ways and my thinking, and I have lived as the subservient female, desiring acceptance and love so much that I lost who I was and my ability to stand up for myself, desperately not wanting to rock the boat and simply did what I was asked.

One evening, as I stood by the stove, I watched my husband add vegetable oil into a pan while preparing dinner. I had been doing a lot of research around the connection of food and the healthy, functional brain and I wanted to do everything I could to help our daughter reach her fullest potential. I was on a mission to put only the best foods into her body and so I had purchased some organic vegetables from a crop share program in our area and I was excited to try okra. But there was a problem. Vegetable oil was not on the list of brain healthy oils recommended for cooking. I knew from my research there were healthier oil options available, and we even had them in our pantry.

As I watched him pour the vegetable oil into the pan, I got angry. My anger was directly related to my fear of where she currently was developmentally versus where I wanted her to be and my desire to make it happen. It made me believe I had to manipulate everything in order to receive the outcome I wanted. From the food she put in her mouth, to the ingredients we used in cooking, and in that moment, even the individual making our dinner; I had to be in control. Trying so hard to control and make sure she had everything she needed, I unleashed a verbal attack on him, communicating that I was obviously the only one who cared about her. Of course, this was the furthest thing from the truth; this was legalistic living at its peak.

At the opposite end of the spectrum was also my desire to please everyone around me and be seen as likeable. One day I took my younger daughter out for some mother-daughter time. I always felt like I struggled to connect with her and due to my insecurity in this, I naturally wanted to make sure I was doing what I could to build our relationship and worked hard trying to make her happy.

For our mother daughter date, I picked my daughter up from school and we went to Sonic to order a couple of drinks on our way to get manicures and pedicures at the local nail salon. We had such a fun time getting pampered while drinking our special drinks and enjoying each other's company. Afterward, we got into the car to go home, but before we were out of the parking lot, she asked if we could also get some ice cream. While her request wasn't out of the ordinary and I did consider it since it was our special day, I decided against it and told her no. I reminded her we had just enjoyed our drinks while getting our nails done and explained it was time to go home. She wasn't happy.

This is where I saw the truth about myself and the happiness of others. I wanted my daughter to like me so much that I was willing to do anything for her. I wanted her to be happy. But what I saw on this outing was the truth that I don't have that sort of power. I can lay myself down and do all the things that another person wants, but they will still ask for more if they are not satisfied. I can give and give to those around me, but at the end of the day, my giving will never be enough to fill another human being. When I am acting out of my fears, I allow others to control me because I want so badly to be accepted myself. But again, living like this allows my fear to have the upper hand.

The problem with either of these extremes is that both lead us to a place of unrest, where we are being controlled by our fears. Someone explained it to me using the example of a pendulum. A pendulum swings back and forth between two end points with its resting point in the middle. Naturally, when we sway between one end or the other, we are not at rest but being pulled back and forth by a force. Recognizing this force is essential as we work to move forward. Without recognizing the forces of fear and our tendencies to react to them, we will struggle, but when we find the middle ground, we find rest and we also find room to grow.

As I have pursued finding this middle ground in my own life, I have come to see that first, God did not design me to be a doormat. God has shown me quite clearly that just as Jesus didn't allow others to walk over him, neither am I to allow others to walk over me. Throughout the Bible others didn't always agree with Jesus and his actions, yet he moved forward anyway. Time and again religious leaders questioned his motives. They ridiculed him for healing people on the Sabbath, sitting with prostitutes and tax collectors, and saying he was the Son of God. But each time, Jesus challenged them, and never stopped being who he was based on other people's opinions of him. He was scorned and harassed, and hung on a cross. But even when he submitted to death on the cross he didn't submit to mankind, but to his Father and the mission he was designed to carry out.

At the same time, Jesus has also given me eyes to see that it is not my job to rule over others with an iron fist. In fact, it is Jesus who reminds those of us who are ready to cast stones, that we have no room to do so, for we too have fallen short of God's glory (Romans 3:23). Recognizing these two extremes, swinging from being a doormat, to ruling over others with an iron fist, has been essential as I fight to overcome my battle with fear, because when I don't see them, I continue to live my life controlled by Satan and live separated from God.

Despite knowing the truth about Jesus, for many years I lived believing that what happened to my daughter was a product of my sin. Because I grew up with God being portrayed as an angry God who disciplines those he loves, usually through painful punishment for wrong doings, it was natural for me to believe that what happened to my daughter was punishment and discipline from God for my sin. Unfortunately however, this belief of mine didn't stop with me.

My beliefs about God and his punitive ways became the standards I used to measure others. Under this judgement I believed, I too became judgmental. If you weren't following the right way, according to what I believed was right, you were wrong. It was black and white. I'd cruelly look down my nose when I saw someone doing something I believed was wrong. After all, I believed they weren't living up to Biblical standards. But guess what, neither was I. I lived in my bubble believing that since I wasn't as 'bad' or 'wrong' as them, I fit into the tidy little Christian box I had built. But what I was actually doing was propping myself up to feel better about who I was in order to feel superior even though me looking down my nose at others was really more about my inadequacies than theirs.

When fear rules our lives, we see God through fear too. But there isn't room for faith when we live this way. God tells us to "be strong and courageous" and to "not be afraid" (Joshua 1:9). He also tells us that fear is not from him (2 Tim. 1:7). Reading through Timothy Jennings' book, *The God-Shaped Brain*, this truth, to choose faith over fear, hit me hard.[2] For the first time, I was able to really understand why faith is so essential to living a full life. Throughout the book Jennings, who is a Christian psychiatrist, talks about how our belief in a God that is scary versus one that is loving and cares for us is detrimental to the human brain.

---

2 Timothy Jennings, *God Shaped Brain: How Changing Your View of God Transforms Your Life* (Downers Grove: IVP Books, 2017).

Because the purpose of fear is to protect us from harm, then viewing God as a harsh judge hinders our ability to draw near to him—the very One who desires to set us free from the hurts we have experienced in our lives. Just as my brain initially detached from my second daughter in an effort to provide me protection upon her birth, we too detach from God to stay safe, just like Adam and Eve did.

As I continued reading Jennings' book and considered this, I thought, *wow, if we are afraid to share our faults and also fear God's condemnation, we are screwed!* Even though Jesus shed his blood for us, and in his great love, takes on the full weight of our sin, there will always be a disconnect if we can't fully accept the truth that God is love. Living with the belief that God is wrathful continues the cycle of shame and keeps us in hiding even while this is exactly the opposite of what God desires for us. He even tells us that only when we hold to his teaching will we know the truth and be set free (John 8:30–32). Just as Adam and Eve had to be honest and courageous in light of their mistakes, and come out from hiding in order to receive God's healing, so do we, to find the mental freedom God desires us to have. Taking this step and exposing our sin requires a willingness to be seen without our fig leaves, and through our honesty and faith, trust that God will protect us against the devil's schemes (Ephesians 6:10–17).

When Jesus was in Gethsemane the night before his death "he fell to the ground and prayed that if possible the hour might pass from him. '*Abba*, Father,' he said, 'everything is possible for you. Take this cup from me. Yet not what I will, but what you will'" (Mark 14:35–36). In his darkest hour, even when asking God to take it from him, Jesus still had faith in the Father's plan. The plan that he knew required him to die, the plan that required the ultimate discomfort and vulnerability. Telling and owning our stories can feel so extremely vulnerable it's tempting to stay quiet. But this is exactly what the enemy wants because as long as we remain afraid, he wins and we remain imprisoned all the while imprisoning others too.

In *Rising Strong*, Brené Brown talks about vulnerability like this, "Vulnerability is not winning or losing; it's having the courage to show up and be seen when we have no control over the outcome. Vulnerability is not weakness; it's our greatest measure of courage."[3] If we are to find freedom, we must die to our flesh. We must begin to believe that our freedom comes when we lay down our fear and the things we believe are protecting us, and trust not in our own understanding, but in God's. We must believe what

---

3 Brené Brown, *Rising Strong: The Reckoning. The Rumble. The Revolution.* New York: Spiegel & Grau, 2015), 4.

the Bible tells us—that God is for us, not against us; that his plan is to prosper, not harm us; and that he desires to take away the yoke of oppression that is holding us down.[4]

Fear will not tell us these things. Fear will tell us to hide, convince us that what we have done is our fault, and that no one will believe us if we tell the truth. Fear will convince us that silence is where we have control, when the truth is that we are the ones being controlled. Yes, it is scary! But finding the courage to take that step of faith will lead to freedom and truth.

I believe we will only find healing and life when we peel off the fig leaves that hide our nakedness before the Father and allow him to break us free from our fear and shame. Breaking free is hard work, but in choosing to do the hard work of uncovering the fear and lies which hold us down, we can stop the cycle that would otherwise leave our kids and loved ones susceptible to the same struggles and burdens which have wreaked havoc on us. When we choose to do the hard work and expose what is true over the lies we believe, we not only free ourselves, but we also free those whom we love. Now let's look at some of the lies we hear.

---

4 See Deuteronomy 31:6; Romans 8:31; Jeremiah 29:11; Isaiah 58:6.

Chapter 5

Lies We Believe

WHEN WE ARE CONTROLLED BY SATAN'S MANIPULATION and lies, we listen to him tell us who we are and our focus turns to outward things. Maybe we work tirelessly to please others, maybe we focus too much on our appearance, maybe we nod our heads when we shouldn't so we won't rock the boat. However it plays out we end up focusing on what is seen and things we believe we can control. But in doing this, we also unfortunately end up putting this focus onto others. As we work harder and harder to live up to the idea of who we believe we should be in order to be accepted, we deny our true selves and create a world more and more intolerant to anyone who lives authentically in who they are and were made to be. When we focus on outward things, authenticity can feel like a threat and something we need to stifle in order to keep going. This is one of the many ways Satan, the whisperer of lies, deceives.

Satan knows if one person believes his lies others will follow, because as humans we influence each other. What we believe to be true in our own minds affects what we say and how we interact with those around us. This is why we must strive to be aware of whether the thoughts inside our minds are speaking truth or telling lies. Recognizing the difference between truth and lies is essential if we are going to break free from the chains that are holding us down and putting us in harm's way.

For many years Satan's lies were pervasive in my life. It wasn't until I was willing to stop focusing on the outward and trust who God made me to be that I was able to start living authentically. And as a result, allow others to do the same. Let's take a closer look at just a few of the lies Satan often uses against us.

Lie: Staying Quiet Equals Staying Safe—Don't Rock the Boat

Oftentimes when we experience trauma, whether as children or adults, we make a silent pact that says we will never be controlled in that way again. We then do everything we can to take life into our own hands. The unfortunate truth in living this way however, is that we are once again being controlled. We become slaves to fear, which tells us we'll be in control if we do this or don't do that.

When I was young, I made several of these pacts. One of those pacts was to stay silent. After seeing what occurred when people get angry and being afraid of that anger, I made the conscious decision to simply not rock the boat. I believed that if I stayed quiet little to no harm would come my way.

But instead of protecting me, my silence rendered me an easy target. "She won't tell anyone," "She won't say anything," "She won't say no," and it was true. I became a doormat, available to take the harm of others and consequently, grew up way too early.

I was unaware that my people-pleasing-don't-rock-the-boat mentality was unhealthy and did not protect me from harm's way. In fact, that mindset was the very thing placing me onto the path of destruction. Each time, in an attempt to stop whatever problem was happening, I took the path of least resistance. I did anything to not feel the weight of another person's anger. In my attempt to keep the peace, I carried the weight of other people's fear, guilt, and shame. I took blame that was never mine to shoulder.

Of course, the problem with taking blame that isn't yours is that it adds up over time, and inevitably, no matter how much you try otherwise, it will overflow.

In my case, I began to suffer great mental duress after so many years of staying quiet. While I had suffered as a child with some anxiety on a couple of occasions, it became more and more intense as I held to the belief that it was my job to keep the peace. The longer I stayed silent, agreeing that things were indeed my problem to deal with, letting others put their own fears and shame on me, the more damage my mind suffered. When we were given the news that our daughter had suffered a traumatic brain injury, I shattered into a million pieces. If all these other things were my fault, how could this be any different? Once again, I took on the blame. Only this time it was too much. My brain couldn't handle the weight anymore and collapsed under the intense pressure. Depression, PTSD, and anxiety took over. I had given my voice away, convinced that silence would protect me. But it didn't. It did exactly the opposite.

Lie: A woman's role is to take care of others and make them happy.

For years I lived believing my role was to make my husband happy. I believed my duty was to him and him alone.

As a Christian woman, I believed that God's desire was for me to "submit" to him. I was told this from the pulpit, saw it in the Bible, and witnessed it as I grew up. The standards and expectations put on me, and that I tried to uphold, were very much the expected duties of a 1950's housewife. I would walk on eggshells trying to make sure my husband was comfortable and happy all the time. The kitchen was to be clean and the food on the table by 6 p.m. when he arrived home from work. If I missed these things he would become a not-so-happy, agitated spouse. I didn't want that, so I played my part and attempted to keep the peace. Additionally (and because my husband was our family's sole provider) my creativity was only valuable if it was bringing in additional income. As a result, I would often choose to only work on my creative projects while he was at work to protect myself from what felt like his judgement over my time management.

I felt like I was doing something wrong when I would choose to use my time for creative expression over cleaning the house or preparing the evening meal. In my mind, as a wife I was supposed to fall under my husband's authority. So this meant if he wasn't happy with me because I was doing something creative, that I needed to put myself aside because his needs were more important. Not putting him first meant I wasn't only going against my husband, but against God as well. I felt so guilty. Was I doing something wrong? Trying to be whom he thought, whom we both thought I was supposed to be, while also wanting to be my real self was hard and it was breaking our marriage. I was trying to do the right thing, so I stayed compliant for a long time. But in doing this, I suffered and lost who I was.

Lie: I'm only as good as my achievements.

So many of us really struggle with putting too much credit into what others say or don't say about us. We might have a few friends and loved ones around us who accept us as we are, regardless of our achievements. But even with this, there are still voices—other's and our own—that criticize, give looks and judgmental glances, pick at, or even deliberately insult that make us doubt the truth of our makeup, design, and worth. Weighed down by the sea of these internal and external voices, we start to listen, and eventually agree.

Because our personal beliefs often become what we project onto others and since we affect each other, we must be careful to question where we are coming from before we speak. If we don't, we risk causing others needless suffering while also causing them to question who God created them to be.

From the time I was little I had big dreams and a variety of creative aspirations, one of which was to be a singer. However, I was told I was not a natural, and only vocalists born with innate talent could make it in the music industry. In addition to that, I lacked in book-smarts as well and was just an average student. The standards around me were high so I struggled to see that my life held any value. If I wasn't smart enough and I wasn't creative enough, what was I? Would I ever be able to measure up? When I started looking toward college, internally, I knew music and art came more naturally to me and captured my attention over scholastic studies. But in the eyes of my parents, they weren't stable enough avenues to stake my future on.

As I began thinking about a college major I remember wanting to major in Voice. In talking through this big decision with my parents I remember my father encouraging me to major in Music Business saying, "You need to be able to get a job when you graduate." Still well into my don't-rock-the-boat ways, I didn't fight it. I went with his recommendation despite my ambitions, deciding I would minor in Voice.

I auditioned for private lessons, a necessary task for those majoring and minoring in Voice at the collegiate level but lacking the classical training most had already received by this point, I was quickly dismissed. "Maybe my dad is right," I told myself. Maybe Voice wasn't for me. So, I took the safe route and majored in Music Business upon being accepted to Anderson University.

But I wasn't ready to give up. During my sophomore year I auditioned once again for Voice, still wanting to minor in it. Again, I was denied. Wanting to improve, I asked the professor I auditioned for what I needed to do to refine my vocal skills. After I had performed a couple of songs for him, he shared with me that if I would sing classical music with the same confidence I was able to sing Broadway show songs, I might have a chance. He then asked me if I had ever considered Belmont University—a school esteemed for their Commercial Voice major and minor. This was something I had never considered and didn't even realize such a school was available. Later on I looked up where the school was and saw it was in Nashville, Tennessee—the land of music. I was excited. Determined to be on the stage believing my value and worth came from proving myself successful in this area, I called my parents and asked if I could audition and possibly transfer to Belmont. To my delight they agreed, but I found myself disappointed when, yet again, I failed to be accepted.

I was defeated. I decided to finish out my Music Business major, but my heart was still in the arts so in my junior year in addition to my existing major, I enrolled in the art program. If I couldn't sing, then I would do art. I was always interested in graphic design and figured it was worth a try. Plus it would provide me with a creative job I would enjoy post college.

So, I became a freshman and a junior at the same time. From the very first class however, I was able to see I was not a natural. As I read through the course descriptions of the requisite 101 and 102 drawing classes needed to progress into the digital realm of a Visual Arts major, I believed I couldn't, and wouldn't, measure up. I knew my skills lacked in comparison to my classmates. My early studio drawings were on par with a beginning elementary age art student, not a college level illustrator. As I hung my work in front of a class of students who had obviously been drawing much longer than myself, each week I would shrink a little more during our critiques.

I lasted one semester in the art department. It never occurred to me that it was okay to be a beginner and that I was there to learn and could learn if I had given myself the chance. In my head, someone with these skills was simply a natural. I was unable to see or accept that maybe there was a time each of my classmates had also been beginners.

At this point, I just wanted to graduate with a degree, but the lie that I was only as good as my achievements was cemented. I wasn't intelligent in the way intelligence is measured and I wasn't a prodigy in music or art. It was all or nothing for me, and I was nothing. I was a mistake. A misfit destined to fail. School was obviously not for me. It never had been. I called home in tears, but my father told me if I wanted to come home and work at the mall for the rest of my life I could. The message was loud and clear: college was the only route to a worthy life.

Externally, I persevered. But inside self-doubt ruled my being. I did what I needed to do to get by, but the little self-confidence I had was shattered. Upon graduating I landed a job because it was expected. My job working in a small print shop typesetting business cards and brochures for local businesses was mindless for the most part. While I viewed the work as an opportunity to grow my knowledge in graphic design, an area I was still interested in, I didn't believe my job was important. Important jobs came with salaries and benefits. My job had no benefits and was hourly. It was the same sort of mall job I had been warned about that night on the phone. To me, I was nobody. But to everyone else, I had graduated from college, had a job, and they were happy. This is all that really mattered however—what everyone else thought of me and my achievements.

Lie: I have to be perfect

This final lie is in some ways tied to everything else we've already discussed. When our identity is tied to the clothes we wear, the possessions we own, the jobs we hold, the behaviors of the kids we are raising, our status within the community we live, or what others think about us, our value and worth become tied up in something other than God and who he says we are. Not only do we lack the ability to accept ourselves as we've already discussed, but we also struggle to accept others for who they really are and measure them by our own flawed expectations. We tell them and show them they are only as valuable and worthy as their accomplishments, looks, income, kids' behavior, and so many other things.

This was my reality for many of the earlier years of raising my daughter with special needs. I remember when she was in kindergarten sitting at the kitchen counter, me hovering over her trying so hard to help her stay on the lines as she traced over letters of the alphabet. I would spend hours (hours!) working with her on these homework practice sheets. I would get so angry. All she had to do was trace the letters. It seemed so simple and yet she was not able to do it. I'd yell at her and say things like, "Why can't you do it?" There were so many things she couldn't do, and we lacked the knowledge of just how severe her delays were.

In addition to me not being able to help her with this aspect of her delays, I was also getting phone calls from the teacher sharing the disheartening news that my daughter was suffering bathroom accidents—on the floor—in the classroom. Even though I knew she was still not potty trained, regardless of my relentless attempts to help her learn this skill and was wearing pull-ups because she simply could not grasp this developmental milestone, I was mortified. Not knowing what else to do, I resorted to disciplinary actions in an attempt to teach her the lesson. I'd take play dates, toys, and snacks away from her. I was clueless that it wasn't behavior modification that was needed.

She couldn't help any of it and I was a mess of a person feeling the pressure to answer questions like, "What's wrong with her?" and "Why aren't you parenting her better?" As I saw ridicule on the faces of other parents, I internalized it and as a result I was also ridiculing, and I directed this at my daughter. I yearned to look good in the eyes of those around me, and to the detriment of my own child, I did it by trying to make her measure up and meet standards that she was incapable of meeting. None of it was about her, it was all about me.

The fact of the matter is the lies and beliefs we hold often become the very judgements we place on others. When we do this, we find ourselves entangled in a web that works against, not with, God. Though the prince of darkness wants us to believe it, "our struggle is not against flesh and blood, but against the rulers, against the authorities, against the powers of this dark world and against the spiritual forces of evil in the heavenly realms" (Ephesians 6:12). Until we begin to do the work of understanding why we believe what we do and from where our beliefs are derived, we will likely continue to place blame and judgement on those in our families, churches, and communities.

Once I started to identify the lies I'd been holding on to for much of my life and realized that they were not helping me, but actually causing great harm to both myself and my family, I started doing the work of journeying out from under them. Journeying isn't always easy, but it's the only way we can move forward and break free so we can start to really live life, a life of freedom.

THEN I HEARD THE VOICE OF THE LORD SAYING,

Whom

I shall ?

send

who will go for us?

AND I SAID, *Here am I.*

Send me.

ISAIAH 6:8

Chapter 6

My Journey Out: Breaking Free

IT WAS OBVIOUS THAT HOW I HAD BEEN LIVING WASN'T working. Simply put, I was a yes girl. I didn't speak up for myself and pretty much just did things for the sake of others. "Whatever you ask, I'll do," was my mantra, but it was clear this was not serving me or those around me. I was at the bottom and I had nowhere else to go, but I wanted to fight for my family and for my daughters. So, slowly, I started to do the work.

One of the ways God started leading me was through the realization that I simply needed to ask for help and trust he would guide me along the way. One of the stories he used that helped me realize this was the story of the Israelites' exodus out of Egypt to the promised land. This account, told in the book of Exodus, tells us of the deliverance of God's people from their slavery in Egypt. The expectations they lived under were demanding and harmful. While the Israelite people wanted to escape this place of torment, it was not an easy thing to do because this life was what they had always known. To go against their enemy required them to stand in opposition and risk what they believed to be true—that it was safer to stay where they were than to follow an unknown path. But this is exactly what God was calling them to do and it was their decision to make (Exodus 1-15).

As God gently taught me the principles in this story and how they also applied to me, I started to see that so many of the "truths" I had believed all my life, were not truths at all, but lies. They were the very things keeping me in oppression. Until I was ready, and my discomfort was more than I could bear there was no reason for me to change. But when the voices inside my head became all-consuming, I was finally in a position to take action. Yes, I was scared. Yes, it was foreign. But at this junction in the road I had a choice to make. I could stay in a place that kept me shackled or I could trust God would go with me and lead me to safety. I knew what I needed to do first, so I reached out to find a counselor.

Moses was the one God sent to lead his people out of Egypt and through the desert toward their promised land. He was the one the Israelites had to trust to lead them on their journey to freedom, regardless of their fears. I too had to choose to trust my counselor as she became the Moses of my story. Through her I started to navigate the untamed landscape of my own impoverished life and fight the battles and enemies that had held me down for so long.

As she led, I had to trust that God was using her to help lead me to freedom. I had to trust when she recommended prescription medicine. I had to believe when she handed me a list of psychiatrists' names, the one with availability would be the right doctor for me. I had to trust that I could speak openly with each of these individuals and it was safe to share the thoughts going on inside my head so they could provide me with the correct therapies and resources to fight the wars battling within me. Over time, I came to learn these wars included depression, anxiety, PTSD, OCD, and intrusive thoughts.

It was all foreign territory. The voices inside my head tried to stop me at each and every junction with more fear and more lies, but each time I took a step forward I was met with the help I needed. It wasn't a straight line from point A to point B, but neither was the journey from Egypt to the promised land. However, this was the very journey I needed to take to find freedom from what had been keeping me chained down for so many years over my life.

Breaking the Silence — Counseling

As I started seeking freedom from my depression and intrusive thoughts, my counselor worked with me using a method called EMDR (Eye Movement Desensitization and Reprocessing).[5] Through this technique, I would focus on an external stimulus (such as a flashing light) that would cause my eyes to move laterally, a musical sound that would rotate from left to right through headphones, or a device that would pulsate from side to side in the palm of my hands. As my mind focused on the sight, sound, or feeling, my therapist would then ask me questions pertaining to the traumas I had endured in my life. This process brought up truths I had suppressed, as well as ones I didn't want to say out loud. Shame, guilt, and fear were vastly present throughout this journey and yet, over time, it

---

5 For more information about EMDR visit www.emdr.com.

provided so much mental freedom from these stored fears and experiences.

During one particular session I shared with my counselor the fact that I had a visceral fear of using public bathrooms. It was so bad I would beg my husband to stand right outside the door and wait for me. In addition to this overwhelming fear, I was also having nightmares of men walking in and violating my privacy while using the facilities. It was obvious to me something was not right, but I couldn't get past whatever was going on inside my brain.

So to bring to light whatever was going on, we began the journey using EMDR. As my therapist took me through a series of different memories my brain would jump from one memory to the next without any rhyme or reason. I didn't understand how they were all connected until I was suddenly back in the hospital, in a white-tiled room, alone with a male interrogation officer sitting across the room from me asking me questions about the hours leading up to my daughter's brain injury.

Suddenly I understood. Every public bathroom I went into had white tiled walls, and that officer, just doing his job, asking me question after question in those traumatic hours, represented the men in my nightmares. Being interrogated along with the trauma my daughter experienced, had traumatized me. That tiled room and the fear I felt within those four walls as he questioned me was recorded inside my brain, specifically my amygdala, which we will discuss more later.

Unable to process or understand my fear of that experience, my brain recorded the sights, sounds, and feelings surrounding that event, and then in an effort to protect me, sounded its alarm with every similar encounter from that point forward. Until I worked through understanding what was happening to me, I was being controlled by my fear. Getting past this and the many other stored traumas I carried, meant showing up and telling the truth of each story that came to mind through EMDR regardless of my fear of judgment.

As I found the courage to share with my therapist and doctors what was going on, more EMDR work was done, medicine was prescribed, and help was given. Over time I learned, over and over again, that everything I was experiencing was associated with my traumatic past. Without knowing it, my past had been controlling me for years. I already knew it was a battle, but now I was also able to see that the only way to truly overcome it was to let go of my net of protection—my silence—and speak the truth out loud to the team of professionals God had placed around me.

Don't Back Down: Setting Boundaries

One of the hardest lessons on my journey toward freedom has been learning how to stand up for myself. To do this I've had to learn skill sets and character traits I lacked. Traits like speaking up even when it is difficult or might rub another person the wrong way, asking for help from those who are educated and experienced in areas I am not, and setting healthy boundaries that inform others how they can and can't treat me. Doing these things has given my spirit room to grow and flourish and as a result, I have been able to keep my demons at bay and resist taking on others' demons as my own. Learning to speak up and set boundaries has not come easy and it has tested my faith in extreme ways, making me rely deeply on the God who tells me he will not leave me nor forsake me, and stretching my faith and belief in him and his Word.[6]

Recognizing that my habit of cowering in the face of fear was not only harming me, but also keeping others from facing their own issues has been invaluable to me.

---

6 Hebrews 13:5-6.

Had I not faced my personal history, I would not have had the strength to live as the person I am rather than the person I believed I needed to and should be. I wouldn't be the wife or mother my family needs which is my true and honest self. Along the way I have had to confront family, friends, neighbors, and even my husband. It has not been easy, but it has been worth it.

I remember distinctly the day I laid down the ground rules within my own marriage. For years I had been going through the motions and playing the role of the subservient wife as I had been taught. It was all I knew. At this point I was several years into my journey out from under all the strongholds I had been living with for so long. I was receiving medical care, individual therapy, and we had both attended marriage counseling at points along the way. It was a long road, but I was taking all the necessary steps toward healing, making sure to take care of my mind, body, and spirit. However, I was still stuck and unable to make forward progress as the being God created me to be. I couldn't understand why until I started to challenge the belief my husband held to be true: I was broken.

One evening however, I took a big step forward. Yes, I was doing all the work. But I was also still living trying to please my husband and keep him comfortable. Standing up to him meant facing my own personal giant—anger—which was something I didn't want to do. But I could see that all of my hard work would be worthless if I didn't put what I was learning into action and continued to play the role of the victim. On this evening, we were having a discussion on our back patio. I was in tears, as was often the case, hearing that I was still broken. As I sat there listening to what he was saying, it dawned on me that he understood my brokenness to be a sign of weakness. But what I had been learning through counseling was that my state of brokenness was a recognition and acknowledgment of my story; it was not weakness, it was strength. I was living my life out from under the fig leaf, but he was still staying behind his. What we both hadn't known, and I was just starting to realize, was that his belief about my brokenness was contributing to my inability to stand, and I was allowing it to keep me down.

It was during this aha moment that I asked him to go back to counseling with me, as we hadn't been going together for some time. He didn't want to. He felt it was my counselor who had broken me. While counseling had indeed broken me from things such as my pride, shame, guilt, and fear these were not negative things. So I asked him a few questions. "What's wrong with being broken?" "Do my tears make me a weaker person?" "Do you see yourself as the strong one and me as the weak one?" He sat in silence. After it became clear he wasn't able to answer I left the conversation angry that I wasn't going to receive answers that evening.

The next day, after I had some time to think about the previous evening's conversation, I sat down and wrote a letter to him spelling out what was okay and wasn't okay for me when it came to our relationship. My pain point was to communicate that I would no longer live allowing him to tell me that I was the weak one and he was the strong one. My silence was holding me back and keeping me from being me and it was time to stop. I sat on the letter for about a week after writing it, not sure how it would come across. I was no longer mad, but I was learning that a boundary not spoken was a boundary not made so I finally gave it to him a week later. That letter was the catalyst to many changes in our relationship, and though it takes a long time to overcome patterns established over seventeen years of marriage, as we work together, our relationship is changing for the better.

Writing that letter sent me down a path of recognizing that in continuing to make my husband comfortable and happy, I was harming myself. I was allowing his pride, fears, and insecurity to control me. What I hadn't allowed myself to realize was the fact that his anger, the force that kept me at bay, was actually not about me. He had his own demons, but they were coming out sideways. His intent was never to harm me or keep me from becoming who I was designed to be. His reactions were from his brain's fight response, a natural, subconscious mechanism, aimed at keeping us safe. But by not facing his fight reaction and with me not facing my flight reaction, neither of us were helping the other. We were both at fault. But even more so, the enemy, the one set on destroying everything on our path, including our marriage, was to blame.

As a woman I grew up believing my responsibility was to man. But as I began the hard work of tearing down the wallpaper of lies in my brain, I began to see God's story differently. Yes, I do have a responsibility to my husband. I was designed to be his helper. But so much of the time our human description of what it looks like to be a helper versus God's intended design gets messed up as we walk through this life. For me, prior to understanding my role under the authority of God, being a helper meant I was responsible for making sure my husband was always at ease. To make sure that dinner was on the table, the house was clean, sex was given, the kids were well behaved, and that I couldn't live as the woman I felt I had been designed to be because it made my husband uneasy. For years I lived this life.

I always struggled to believe God would be mad at me if I didn't do what my husband told me to do because I knew it was one of God's "rules." But then one day I saw the story of Mary and Joseph in a different light and realized God's desire was for me to follow him and allow him to have the ultimate authority.

When we look at Mary's story, God tells her she will become pregnant. In hearing him, she simply responds, "I am the Lord's servant. May your word to me be fulfilled" (Luke 1:38). However, when Joseph, a worthy and upright man, finds out the news, he plans to leave her in order to protect his reputation. Through this immaculate conception God appears to Joseph in a dream and tells him not to be afraid saying, "She will give birth to a son, and you are to give him the name Jesus, because he will save his people from their sins" (Matthew 1:21). Through this dream, Joseph stays.[7]

Nowhere in the story of Mary & Joseph, does it show or say that it was Mary's responsibility to keep Joseph reassured, or to protect him in any way, yet this is the message

---

7 Read the whole story in Matthew 1:18–25.

I grew up hearing and believing. A message that, to this day, continues to be taught to boys and girls everywhere.

Mary, the mother of Jesus and God's chosen recipient to birth new life had one Being whom she was responsible to—God. Her job as his chosen daughter was to obey him and to birth the child who would reconcile mankind to God himself. Joseph, too, had a responsibility. His responsibility to God's call was to watch over both Mary and the baby to come, regardless of the criticism or opinions of others and this is exactly what he did. He risked his character for the sake of protecting the woman pledged to be his wife, heeding God's direction to lead.

What I have now come to learn however, is that my relationship with him as a "submissive" wife—doing what he desired when he desired it—was not helping him. In fact, it was hurting him. My fear of his reaction was my god. In bowing to my insecurities, I was not living out the life God desired me to live. God calls me to not bow to my fears and insecurities, but to stand up not only to the demons running my life, but to the demons running my husbands, and also encourage him and stand beside him as he does the same. In not following God's command to not be afraid, I threw my husband under the bus. I made him a victim to the enemy's attacks just as Eve did. But when

I learned to stand my ground, believing God over Satan's lies, and being accountable to God above all else, I made a way for us to find life. Through my example, my husband was able to stand up too, and seek the help he needed from the enemies controlling his own mind.

In standing up, I have come to learn the best way I can help my husband, and my family, is to submit to God and take the actions necessary to be who he asks me to be, not who the world or those around me believe I should be. In being true to what God has designed me to be, I am able to help my husband in his own fight and the war he faces. The war which tells him he is alone, and it is all on his shoulders. Carrying this weight and pressure exacerbates fear. In these instances, a man needs a woman who will not cave to his fear. When one spouse is stuck in fear, the other spouse can come beside them, strong in their faith, living under God's authority, to help lead them as a partner, to the One who can relieve us of the burdens we carry along the way. We all have something in our lives we need to stand up to. For me, this played out in my relationships. For you, it may play out differently. But over everything, when we stop letting lies rule and let God rule instead, we find the freedom and grace to be our unique, true selves, which is what God designed us to be.

Owning My Story: Grace.

Prior to doing the hard work of cleaning out the clutter which filled my life, I saw myself as someone who had it all together. But as I sat in my therapist's office and aired the dirty laundry of my past, laying it out on the table before me, I was forced to confront my downfalls. I came to see that I haven't done anything perfectly and yet, God sent his Son so my sins would be forgiven. God loves me just as I am, flaws and all. I am forgiven. Yes, a lot of my past was done to me, but a lot of it is also a product of choices I made. Until I was brought face to face with this truth, I hid. And in my hiding, I lived believing I was better than others.

The problem with believing this, however, is that no one is capable. Each of us sin daily in this broken world. Our salvation is by grace and grace alone. Until we see this and know it for ourselves, we risk striking down others who are struggling and become incapable of being the hands and feet of Christ. Under this belief system we become ambassadors of the enemy rather than Christ, and it becomes extremely difficult to truly show the attributes of Jesus—compassion, empathy, unconditional love, acceptance, and grace—because we are living out of just the opposite, judgement. The Bible is clear in telling us that until we remove the plank from our own eyes, we have no right removing it from those around us.[8] Sadly, many never do the hard work of looking inward, yet this is where we must begin if we are to affect positive change, first in ourselves, and then in the people and world around us.

As a parent, it's so easy to let my insecurities tell me that if my children don't behave or speak in the manner considered appropriate by those around me it is a poor reflection on me. Believing this can cause a parent to go to extremes because if our kids don't dress or behave the "right" way, then suddenly we are the ones who receive the raised eyebrows. When we start to absorb these kinds of reactions and let them feed us the lie that we need to be perfect, it's all too easy to start thinking we need to change our kids. But this isn't really about our kids at all, it's about us and our own insecurities and about the insecurities of those doing the judging.

---

8 See Matthew 7:5.

My time in the trenches with my daughter has taught me I do not have the power to change anyone. I only have the ability to change my own behaviors toward another being. As I look at my daughter today, I see a beautiful girl who has come a long way. She still has delays and will graduate with a special needs diploma, but I have come to accept where she is. While I still push her wanting the best for her, there are a lot of things I have learned to let go of. One of the biggest being the realization that she may remain forever young. Her mental state is significantly younger in development than her physical age. Though she is seventeen, she still loves and adores her baby dolls and I receive looks because she carries them with her everywhere we go. While this is hardly accepted in our society, I know those dolls are her pride and joy and since she is my pride and joy, the looks don't bother me anymore. Through our struggles together I have come to learn what is true—the glances we receive aren't about us, they are about those who give them.

As I have journeyed out from under all the lies and false beliefs I held for so long, I have slowly found the courage to let go of the fear, to speak things out loud, and to stop trying to do life on my own. I am learning we are not created to do life by ourselves and that even though God is ultimately in control he has given us tools and resources for a reason. In choosing to let go and trust God and those he has put around me for guidance, I continue to find strength to share the hard truths and quiet the loud, abusive voices that were slowly killing me. Little by little, as I trusted and shared, I found I could trust without judgement. With their help, I found compassion, understanding, knowledge, and wisdom. But most of all, I found hope, healing, and life.

Chapter 7

A New Story

I HAVE LONG BEEN IN AWE OVER THE HUMAN BRAIN. Between my daughter's story and my own struggles with depression, anxiety, OCD, intrusive thoughts, and PTSD much of the last sixteen years of my life has been focused around understanding this complex organ. The deeper I peer, the more I find myself asking: Is there a correlation between the wiring of the human brain and one's ability to find new life and freedom from an enslaved mindset?

To answer this question, let's first consider two parts of the human brain: the amygdala and the prefrontal cortex. Located just below the brain stem, the amygdala is the storage center of our emotional memories, specifically those surrounding fear and anger. It controls our inactive thinking (things that run through our brain without a conscious awareness). When triggered by something that threatens our safety, be it another person, an event, or circumstances outside our control, this almond-sized area of the brain will communicate unconsciously with the conscious part of our brain, called the prefrontal cortex.

The prefrontal cortex, located just behind the forehead, is the brain's processing center. It allows us to make decisions while understanding what is happening around us on a conscious level. We use the prefrontal cortex when we engage higher level thinking and reasoning, such as solving a problem or recalling elements of a story, and it controls our active thinking (things we are consciously processing).

When the amygdala is triggered by a traumatic emotional memory, it communicates with the prefrontal cortex and unconsciously communicates we are in danger. This is when fight-or-flight mode, the urge to either fight or flee the perceived danger, kicks in. This is our body's natural defense mechanism.

Unfortunately, because our brains store everything we encounter, the traumas we endure throughout our lifetime can wreak havoc on our daily lives, decisions, and relationships. Given this, it's very easy to make decisions out of the painful parts of our past. When we function out of these hurt places, our brains communicate a story of danger to us in instances that are not necessarily threatening. The result is a life of reacting to the world around us in self-defense instead of being able to get curious and consider the reasons why we behave as we do.

Unresolved traumatic circumstances will control us and those around us if we aren't careful. This is why it is important to do the hard work of understanding emotions such as anger and fear, the two emotions the amygdala is responsible for. Consider my experience with white-tiled public bathrooms. My brain was telling me I was in danger; the emotional memories of my past told me to flee in order to protect myself. But, I wasn't helping myself. I was living my life in constant reaction to my stored emotions and it was stealing life from me.

Which brings us to answer the earlier question: Is there a correlation between the wiring of the human brain and one's ability to find new life and freedom from an enslaved mindset? The answer is yes! If our brains are wired in a way where the negative, undealt with, stored emotions we encounter throughout our lives are processed through the subconscious brain (the amygdala), and our day-to-day functions and behaviors are dictated from our conscious brain (the prefrontal cortex), then we aren't truly living life if we haven't processed these events and happenings.

In my own life, I have come to realize I was living much of my life with no awareness as to why I did the things I did or thought the way I thought. My thoughts were controlling me, and my unconscious self was the decision maker. When I felt fear, I needed to be in control. When I felt shame, I needed to hide. But in becoming aware of these reactions and learning more about why I was doing them, I was able to take some steps forward. Steps that enabled me to let go of my need to be in control while also choosing to reveal things I wanted to hide in order to protect myself. As I started to understand what had been happening inside of me for so long, I was able to start seeing things for what they were—the truth. My actions and behaviors were part of a complex system of traumatic circumstances that had coded my brain. My thoughts became my beliefs and my beliefs became my actions.

This is why it is so important for us to take responsibility for the things in our lives that cause us to build walls of protection in the first place. Until we tear down these walls, not only are we imprisoned within them, but we also end up imprisoning others in the same way. We imprison others when we project our own false beliefs onto those around us. These distorted truths become the weapons we use to keep others at bay. Self-directed anger (also known as depression) and outward anger are often signals encouraging us to take note of what we are believing to be true and that something deeper is occurring inside. If anger is present, since it is most often a secondary emotion, fear, hurt, and shame are likely nearby.

The Bible talks at length about the importance of being aware of those things that are happening inside our minds, as opposed to allowing them to lead the way.[9] It tells us that "the mouth speaks what the heart is full of" (Matthew 12:34). While this can sometimes be difficult to acknowledge, the good news is it doesn't have to stay this way. Once we understand how our thoughts can hold us and others captive, we have the opportunity to make a conscious decision to take action and seek healing. We have the opportunity to come out from behind our fears and shame and from the thoughts holding us captive.

Over the past several years I have worked through the emotional traumas that held me captive for so long. As I continue to heal, I find myself becoming more and more aware of the brutal whispers of the enemy that tell me

9 Matthew 12:33–37; 2 Corinthians 10:5; Philippians 4:8; Romans 12:2; Colossians 3:2; Romans 1:28.

everything is my fault, that I am to blame, that I am bad, and that I'm the problem. Even in the last several months I find myself very attuned to the enemy's lies. At every turn, his lies try to convince me to quit this journey I am on, poking at my fear and shame. In the past lies were a part of my inactive thinking and I would have never noticed them. Recognizing them has been a huge step forward for me. Now I am able to acknowledge them for what they are and speak what I know is true –I am good, valuable, and worthy. I am fearfully and wonderfully made (Psalm 139:14), and God's plans are to prosper me, not harm me (Jeremiah 29:11). I am able to finally believe that his perfect love drives out my fear and shame. His love reminds me I can stand tall in him because I am clean.

In the garden, God created Adam and Eve to live free of fear, shame, and guilt. But once they ate the fruit God told them not to eat, they felt all of those things. They hid from God and passed blame—Adam to Eve, and Eve to the serpent—for their actions. But once they told God the truth, while there were still consequences to their actions and they had to leave the garden, he did not abandon them; he took care of them by clothing them with suitable garments. Satan's aim was destruction, but God still brought redemption. Even though things changed, and sin was now a part of the world, he gave them a way out from under their fear and shame through his love and forgiveness.

God does the same for us. He wants to free us from the chains that weigh us down. He wants us to accept his love and forgiveness. He wants to redeem us and make us whole. But this can only come when we recognize our brokenness and truly surrender our lives to Jesus, just as he did for us on the cross. When Jesus gave his life, he defeated darkness and paid our price; his death allows us to be whole again. Following Jesus's example, we too can bring forth life. Because when we let go of the things that protect us and share our stories, we partner with him in his death and resurrection.

The decisions I make can lead me to life, or they lead me to death. I choose to exercise, despite my desire not to, because I know it helps my brain. Not easy, but worth it. I choose to eat healthier options because I know they fuel my body. Not always easy, but worth it. I choose to sit down and write every day because I have a goal to finish my book. Not easy, but worth it. It's the same with surrendering to God's plan over our own, or telling the truth, over hiding. Not easy, but oh, so worth it. In the end, we reap the consequences of our own actions. We are warned over and over, but we are stubborn and often don't get it.

When we hide because of fear our natural tendencies are to stay quiet and protect ourselves at all cost, even if that cost may be detrimental to ourselves and others. But what I want you to know is this: Speaking the truth and bringing our fear and shame into the light, reduces their power and loosens their control over us. The Bible tells us that the darkness cannot survive the light.[10] The lies we listen to tell us otherwise, so we stay in hiding, ashamed, and distant from God. As we believe the lies of the enemy, we forfeit the life that God so desperately desires us to have.

Maybe for the sake of our livelihood and mental health as well as those around us we could begin to consider a new story. A story that tells us God and his Word has the answers to set us free. It's up to us, will we surrender our lives to him and trust he won't let us fall? Will we live believing that if everything we know is taken from us, he will still be enough? Or will we live in fear that disposing of our masks and revealing the brokenness underneath makes

---

10 John 1:5.

us weak? Even if that means we hurt those around us as we try to keep hiding.

I still so clearly remember when God asked me to lay down everything, other than him, that I had been putting my identity in instead of dealing with my own pain and fear. My husband and I were vacationing on the island of St. Thomas in the Virgin Islands. We left our hotel one morning to go for a run. The heat was stifling but the ocean scenery made it manageable. As we ran along the coast with the ocean on one side of us and rush hour traffic on the other, I focused on the music playing through my headphones. The song "I'm Letting Go" by Francesca Battistelli came on. The song beautifully details what it feels like to loosen the grip of our future by putting the full weight of our tomorrow into God's hands and implicitly trusting he will catch us when we do.

At this point in my life my work and level of success still defined me. It took precedence over my family, because the message I heard and believed was that I was only as good as my successes. The dreams themselves were not bad, but the internal message which drove me to achieve them was unhealthy, hurting both myself and those around me.

As I listened to the words of the song, I lost it. Chills swept over my body as tears poured down my face and mixed with the sweat. In that moment I knew God was asking me to allow him to be enough. So, after years of trying to do it alone, I gave up everything that was defining my life and started a new chapter. A chapter that required me to lay down my fear and shame and pick up a new weapon. The weapon of faith.

I love the parable of the Prodigal Son in Luke 15. It states, "There was a man who had two sons. The younger one said to his father, 'Father, give me my share of the estate.' So he divided his property between them. Not long after that, the younger son got together all he had, set off for a distant country and there squandered his wealth in wild living" (vv.11-13).

In this story we see how the son made the decision to leave his father's house where he had everything he needed. He chose to believe that he could find a more fulfilling life somewhere else. But as we keep reading look how the story unfolds:

> After he had spent everything, there was
> a severe famine in that whole country,
> and he began to be in need. So he went
> and hired himself out to a citizen of that

country, who sent him to his fields to feed pigs. He longed to fill his stomach with the pods that the pigs were eating, but no one gave him anything.

When he came to his senses, he said, "How many of my father's hired servants have food to spare, and here I am starving to death! I will set out and go back to my father and say to him: Father, I have sinned against heaven and against you. I am no longer worthy to be called your son; make me like one of your hired servants." So he got up and went to his father.

But while he was still a long way off, his father saw him and was filled with compassion for him; he ran to his son, threw his arms around him and kissed him.

The son said to him, "Father, I have sinned against heaven and against you. I am no longer worthy to be called your son."

But the father said to his servants, "Quick! Bring the best robe and put it on him. Put a ring on his finger and sandals on his feet. Bring the fattened calf and kill it. Let's have a feast and celebrate. For this son of mine was dead and is alive again; he

was lost and is found." So they began to
celebrate. (vv. 14–24)

Just like the father, God's desire is for us to choose
him. But he allows us to make our own decisions in hopes
that when we go astray and experience losses that often
come as natural consequences to our choices, we will also
choose to return home to God, where he gives us new life.
The father wasn't angry at his son for the choices he made.
He welcomed him home with open arms and celebrated
his return, just as he was. This parable shows us what our
Father feels for us and the abundance of grace, love, and
mercy he has for us when we turn back toward him.

It is hard sometimes to believe that God is for us
and not against us as we travel this path. What I learned
through my own return to letting God lead me that day as
I ran along the oceanside, is that we have to let go of the
things that control us, and trust God is already running to
us, with open arms, in celebration, welcoming us home so
we can start to heal.

There are so many stories of healing sprinkled throughout the New Testament. In each case a hurting individual
comes to Jesus, a father seeking healing for his child; a
woman believing that in simply touching Jesus's cloak she
would find healing; a blind man wanting to see; some men

trying to help their paralyzed friend; each one chose to believe. As I considered Jesus's response to each of them I am in awe. In each instance his reply is, "Your faith has healed you."[11]

Faith. The word was so familiar, but as I really started to think about it, I began to wonder, what is it really? Hebrews 11:1 says this, "Now faith is confidence in what we hope for and assurance about what we do not see." Faith is being confident of what we believe, even when we cannot see it. For years the record in my mind told me I was a failure, the dreams I had were too big, and that I wasn't smart enough or talented enough to be who I dreamed of being; that I was bad. I struggled. How was I to reconcile what I believed about myself with what I also believed was my destiny—a capable daughter of the King, clean and presented without stain or blemish? I couldn't. So, eventually, I finally did what so many of us do. I took matters into my own hands. I carried the burden, all the fear, guilt, and shame alone. It took many years and so much more pain before I was able to see, to believe that God had a different story for me—a new story—and he had been there waiting, with open arms welcoming me home all along.

---

11 Mark 5:21–43; Luke 18:35–42; Mark 2:1–5.

So I want to also ask you: What if we take off our masks and start to look beyond the doubt and fear that goes against our destiny? What if we stop accepting the doubt and fears of others? What if we stop believing all the lies being fed to us? What if instead we choose to have faith that God really does love us deeply and unconditionally as the beings he designed us to be? What will happen?

I believe our faith will heal us and give us the power to overcome the circumstances we face, while bearing the image of God in the presence of our enemies. I believe it, because I have lived it.

When we choose to believe the truth of God, our faith allows us to push through difficult circumstances because we know he is with us, crying with us, standing with us, speaking out truth, covering our shame with his love, defeating the darkness, defeating the grave, giving us a new story—giving us life.

"In all this you greatly rejoice, though now for a little while you may have had to suffer grief in all kinds of trials. These have come so that the proven genuineness of your faith—of greater worth than gold, which perishes even though refined by fire—may result in praise, glory and honor when Jesus Christ is revealed" (1 Peter 1:6–7).

Conclusion

Beautifully Broken

As I work through my story and rumble with the hardships this life has dealt me, I sometimes feel sad for my younger girl because I know the world she encounters and attempts to work through is downright harsh. For many years I lived with the mindset that it was my special needs daughter who was missing out on the good things. But this is the furthest thing from the truth. My daughter with special needs is the one thriving in the areas of acceptance, value, and worth. She is seen by her peers and those who know her story as the being she is, not the being the world around her says she has to be. This is life! Given her special needs she isn't expected to live beyond what she is capable of doing. But for those of us deemed "normal" by the world's standards, we are expected to not only achieve, but exceed what is put before us. Poor us! Not poor them. We are the ones who live believing the lies that tell us our value is found in what we do, what we achieve, how we look and perform, and how we hold ourselves together along the way. So we live in this weird and difficult dynamic, where we aren't enough and we are too much, all at the same time.

My special needs daughter is in a community of kids who all struggle with differences. But despite these differences, whether emotional, mental, or physical, they are who they are, and they each accept each other regardless. They show up every day, disregarding the barriers that could separate each of them. They recognize somehow that they are all much more alike than different, and they work to champion one another along the way. From where I stand, as the mom of one these special kids, I see they have found the secret to life! They are a team. We "normal" ones could learn from them if we were willing to let down our guards, ask for help, and accept that we can't do everything on our own. But until we are willing to risk our pride and be seen for who we are, over who we believe we have to be for the sake of acceptance and approval, we are the ones missing out.

Unfortunately, what we often experience is seen in the classrooms, hallways, and lunchrooms of our mainstream kids where peers don't always root each other on or accept their downfalls. Instead, they are often seen vying for the rung that hangs a little higher; positioning themselves just so on the ladder of success to keep the ones next to them a little lower. It's disheartening to watch and parent through, let alone fight through it as an adult. We think our middle school days are behind us once we are grown. Yet we often find ourselves still facing the same battle with our friends, co-workers, relatives, and community while struggling to see that behind all the facades are scared, lonely people doing their best to find acceptance for who they are, not what they do.

I learned a valuable lesson one day during an impromptu play session with my younger daughter. She was four at the time and was pretending to be a lion. She was squatting on all fours low to the ground hunting pillows as her prey. As she played, I picked up a pillow and threw it over to the side and said, "Get that one. It's all alone."

As the words left my mouth, my spirit was struck. God was revealing this truth to me: We become the enemy's prey when we are left to do life on our own.

As my kids grow, I realize my fears and concerns around loneliness are justified. But I have been worried about the wrong kid. I used to be afraid and think I had to do more to help my special needs daughter build a support group of safety around her, but middle school with my youngest taught me something quite different about the harsh truth of the world we live in. Contrary to what I expected, it isn't my special needs daughter who suffers with loneliness; it is my regular developing girl.

Had I not done the internal work necessary to overcome the fear, guilt, and shame of my own past, my typical developing child would continue to walk without an advocate to quiet the voices telling her she is all alone. Until I faced my own insecurities I was unable to walk with her. Before I did the hard work of journeying out from under everything, unintentionally, I laid the burdens of my fears on her shoulders too and was contributing to her insecurities.

For years my youngest also carried the weight and responsibility of protecting her older sister. I would tell her to watch out for her when they'd have play dates at someone else's house. Until she voiced it out loud, I was unaware of what this did to her. It made her believe that if anything ever happened to her sister, it was her fault. I gave her the same weighted blanket I had carried for years and unknowingly laid it on her shoulders.

In not speaking up I took responsibility for things done to me by others who should have never done them. In not speaking up my daughters both suffered harm. In staying quiet I carried the weight of guilt and shame that was never mine to carry. In carrying my guilt and shame in silence, I also put it onto those nearest and dearest to me. Silence destroys life.

In sharing my story with trusted advisors, I found help and freedom. In speaking up and breaking the chains of people pleasing, I freed myself from the fears and shame of those surrounding me, and found the strength to embark on the journey God was calling me to. In speaking up I became an advocate for both of my children and am teaching them the importance of not staying quiet. In speaking up I became who God designed me to be too.

My special needs daughter is authentic and real. She shines bright in who she is, not in what she does. Her heart, despite her actions at times, is pure. She radiates light and love. She will never meet the standards and expectations of this world or sadly, sometimes even the expectations of the church. But the beautiful reality is we don't expect her to. She lives on the outside what the rest of us live on the inside. She doesn't hide. She lives and loves and finds that some people accept her, while others do not. But she doesn't change who she is as a result of it, nor do I ask her to. She isn't who she is on purpose. She is who she is due to the damage that was done to her. Whether she experienced trauma early in life or not, she would still have pain simply because she was born into this fallen world, just as each one of us does. The blessing she has, however, is that she is given grace by those who know and love her because they know her story and recognize she can't change.

We do not ask our daughter to be anyone other than who she is. There are no standards she is expected to live up to. Instead, we celebrate every milestone. We love, regardless of the quirks, and forgive quickly because we know she is merely broken. In truth, we are all broken. We are all a product of this world and the hurt bestowed upon us and most of us are not afforded the same grace my oldest daughter is. But God gives us grace abundantly. He sees and knows the by-products of all our hurt and pain and just as I completely accept my daughter, God completely accepts us too, just as we are, faults and all.

I'm not perfect but raising a special needs child with brain trauma finally allows me to see that God never expected me to be. I know that the majority of my daughter's behaviors and struggles are a product of the hurt that was done to her. She didn't have a choice; she was only six months old at the time of her injury. As I look at my child and recognize the vast amount of love I have for her, I find myself challenged by the thought: *If I can see my daughter's heart through the mess, cannot God see mine?*

Acknowledgments

To my husband: Thank you for your willingness to stand by me through this journey. You have seen me at my absolute worst, and even then, you chose to stay by my side. You fought for me by owning what was yours and showed me I was worth that battle. There are not many men who would do that. Thank you for showing me what real love is!

To my family: I love you all! Though the journey has been hard, I am now able to see it was necessary. God has delivered me through the murky waters, and I am better off having gone through them. 1 Peter 1:6-7 says it all.

To my tribe: I couldn't have made it through my road to recovery, much less the writing of this book, without each of you. You all know who you are. God knew just the women I needed in my life to walk this road with love and grace. I am incredibly grateful for your friendships.

To my editor: Thank you! Reliving my journey was extremely difficult, but you walked me through it with genuine grace. What I gave you was a mess! But you helped me carve a meaningful treasure out of that pile of words that I can now pass on to my daughters.

To my designer: The very first book I ever wrote I designed myself. It was awful! You have done an amazing job with the cover and interior and I am so grateful for your expertise! Thank you for your incredible skills.

To my beta readers: Thank you for your willingness to read *No Longer A Yes Girl* before it was in book form. Your constructive feedback was invaluable to me.

To Heather and Adonis Lenzy: Thank you both for your wisdom and fire-side talks. Being able to pick the brains of those who have gone before me was incredibly helpful.

To Jeff Goins: Thank you for the work you do. Had it not been for your online class and your TRIBE seminars, I wouldn't be writing this acknowledgment today. I can't believe I actually did it!

About the Author

Rana McIntyre

has been authoring blogs for over seventeen years. What began as an emotional outlet to share the hardships of raising a child with special-needs turned into a life-line of expression. She is a wife and mom of two teenage girls and lives just outside of Nashville, Tennessee. Be sure to stop by RanaMcIntyre.com to learn more.

Made in the USA
Monee, IL
01 February 2021

59041186R00075